Dat

debut

ON TWO

Phillippa Giles and Vicky Licorish are the producers of
the series *Debut on Two*.

Phillippa Giles has worked for the past three years
as a script editor in the BBC's drama department.
Now a producer, she has recently completed the
adaptation of Jeanette Winterson's *Oranges Are Not The
Only Fruit* for television.

Vicky Licorish has worked extensively as an actress,
writer and presenter in films, theatre and television. Her
work as a presenter includes two years on BBC 1's
Saturday Superstore.

debut

ON TWO

A guide to writing for television

EDITED BY PHILLIPPA GILES AND VICKY LICORISH

BBC BOOKS

Published by BBC Books,
a division of BBC Enterprises Limited
Woodlands, 80 Wood Lane, London W12 0TT

First published 1990

ISBN 0 563 20810 4

Set in 10½ on 12½pt Galliard by Ace Filmsetting Limited, Frome, Somerset.
Printed and bound in Great Britain by Redwood Burn Limited, Trowbridge, Wiltshire.
Cover printed by R. Clay & Co., Norwich.

Contents

Introduction

*Phillippa Giles and
Vicky Licorish*

Debut on Two – both the book and the series – aims to inspire new writing for television. By devising the challenge of a fifteen-minute script and throwing the doors open to all comers we ended up with an exciting season of plays that reflect Britain in the late 1980s.

Workshops and writers

We began the search for scripts by advertising widely and organising workshops all over the country: from Glasgow to Belfast. These workshops were designed to get people to analyse the current diet of mainstream television drama and to question the established formulas.

We were accompanied at each workshop by a writer native to that particular community; this encouraged a genuine dialogue between writers 'on the inside' and those who often saw themselves as 'out in the cold'.

Talking to so many different writers and listening to their responses to our guest speakers made us recognise the real need for a contemporary book on television written by writers for writers. It should be said, however, that this book is not a manual on how to write for television. Rather it is a collection of highly individual essays by working writers each suggesting some starting points based on their own experience. These range from very practical advice on script construction (Ray Jenkins: 'Basics') and how and where you can get your script read (Roger Gregory: 'Foot in the Door') to the more personal perspectives on inspiration (Stephen Lowe: 'Breath of Inspiration') and adaptation (Jeanette Winterson: 'Adaptations'). In addition, we have reproduced in full the eight scripts selected for the series with a foreword by our script editor, Hilary Salmon, on why these eight were chosen out of the 3500 scripts we received.

The writers and their chapters

Of the seven writers contributing essays to this collection the first three took part in the *Debut on Two* workshops:

Ray Jenkins participated in the Cardiff workshop and proceeded to enthral the audience with his talk on basic tools for the writer. We are delighted to be able to present these invaluable starting blocks as our opening chapter. Ray is a very experienced television writer with credits stretching from *Juliet Bravo* to his adaptation of *The Woman in White* and, more recently, *The Trial of Klaus Barbie*.

Michael Wilcox, who led our Newcastle workshop, has gone from writing plays like *Rents* and *Massage* for the theatre to equally successful television work such as his *Film on Four: Accounts* and *Lent* for *Screen Two*. Here, he provides an analysis of the difference between film and videotape through focusing on the device of the opening titles.

Next to Ray Jenkins's and Michael Wilcox's contributions we set the startlingly original voice of a relative newcomer: **Iain Heggie**. Iain's credits have been mainly in the theatre with *Politics in the Park*, *American Bagpipes* and *Clyde Nouveau*, but he successfully transferred *Wholly Healthy Glasgow* from the stage to the screen as part of BBC1's *Play on One* 1988 season. Iain's chapter on structure represents a distillation of his Glasgow workshop where he applied the lessons of classic stagecraft to contemporary television drama.

Stephen Lowe, author of stage plays such as *Touched* and *Divine Gossip* and of television work including *Cries from the Watchtower*, *Kisses on the Bottom*, twenty episodes of *Albion Market* and *Ice Dance* for *Screen Two*, has contributed perhaps the hardest essay for any writer on the elusive subject of inspiration.

As well as writers' perspectives, we have also widened our brief to include a chapter from the doyen of comedy producers, **Paul Jackson**. Since the majority of unsolicited scripts sent to the BBC's Script Unit are in the sit-com genre, we thought it important to ask the producer of such seminal television comedy as *The Young Ones*, *Friday Live* and *Red Dwarf* to contribute to a book about writing for television.

No book on writing for television would be complete without a chapter on the art of adaptation. The award-winning young novelist, **Jeanette Winterson**, comes to television with all the trepidation of someone 'busting up' her own novel for the first time. Idiosyncratic and personal, Jeanette's essay sums up this book's overall message: that nobody can tell you how to write; all we can do is provide some individual approaches and leave the rest to your own imagination.

We round off with a chapter on how to get your work noticed, by **Roger Gregory**, now a drama producer, who was for several years senior script editor in Pebble Mill's Drama Unit, working with writers on a whole canon of work including script-editing *The Boys from the Blackstuff*.

Debut on Two – the series

The second half of this book publishes in full the eight scripts we finally selected for the series. This section is introduced with an analysis of how we arrived at these eight plays by our script editor, Hilary Salmon. Hilary came to us having been literary manager at the Royal Court and Liverpool Playhouse, but even she was slightly daunted at the prospect of the 3500 scripts that poured in as a result of our workshops and nationwide appeal for scripts.

Over all we were impressed with the level of competency we found as we ploughed through the sackfuls of submissions. However, too many writers had failed to take up the specific challenge of *Debut on Two* to 'discover new ways of saying things' and fell back too readily on the well-trodden ground of naturalistic drama. At the other end of the spectrum, we had a collection of time-based works from artists working in sculpture and video arts but since, in the end, we were looking for evidence of *good writing*, these too fell by the wayside. Eventually, through a process of continual dialogue and debate between the three of us, we whittled the submissions down to a shortlist of fifty writers, many of whom we met in order to arrive at the final eight whose plays we have commissioned.

Reading many, often very personal, expressions of feeling about the world gave us an invaluable insight into contemporary concerns.

What we noticed most was how the effect of Thatcher's Britain has led to a devolution of collective responsibility. The majority of our writers were writing about their concern for themselves and their families and few attempted a broader perspective.

Debut on Two set out to prove many things but perhaps two of the most important were that there was a wealth of undiscovered writing talent whose voices were not being heard and that television drama could finally lay the ghosts of David Mercer and John Hopkins with pride in a new way forward. The scripts we received asserted very palpably the truth of our first venture and the eight plays published in this volume, we hope, prove the second: that the fifteen-minute play does work as a way of defining a new form for television drama.

Our enthusiasm for the challenge of television drama has been strengthened by the experience of producing this project and we defend television's right in an increasingly hostile environment to go on pursuing new forms, new voices, new writers.

Part 1

Basics

Ray Jenkins

Imperatives

J. B. Priestley once said there are two kinds of writer – those who write and those who just talk about writing. By the latter he didn't mean critics, academics or novice script editors, but those who, after a hard evening in night-school and pub burying Sophocles and Thomas Hardy, went home to sleep, whereas the former picked up their midnight pens and wrote. For those interested, now, in television writing, the distinction would probably be between those who want to say something and those who will say anything in order to get their names on the screen. I'm talking to the former, to those who are excited by the chemistry of words and the craft of putting scripts together, who think television *writing* matters and who regard nightly audiences as worthy of respect. All else is, curiously, vanity.

I have been asked to offer notes on 'basics', so, my first imperative is:

WRITE WHAT YOU WANT TO WRITE

Let it be felt on *your* pulse, let it be about what *you* know, an expression of *your* individuality. If you only start by trying to write what you think others want, then you've sold out before you begin, done a disservice to yourself and television in general, and given those who will sit in judgment on your script the simplest reason for rejection – 'we've heard it all before'. If you have satanic verses in you, speak! Second imperative:

HAVE AN INITIAL DISREGARD FOR PRODUCERS

In your act of creation they come in roughly with the winged fowl on the fifth day. You justify their existence, the exercise of their talent depends on your piece. I repeat, have the confidence at this stage to enjoy what *you* want to say. Compromises will, of necessity, come later, but don't load your back with their problems now. Believe me, good producers, those cherishable few, will be exhilarated by such an attitude; a good script lightens their lives, a bad one wastes everybody's time. Cost has narrowed the potential field for new writing to two expensive areas – film and individual plays, say a few dozen slots. *That* is why you've got to get your voice right. Therefore declare war on cliché. Third imperative:

LET YOUR MODELS BE THE BEST

You want to break into a severely professional world – OK, start working. Watch reputable work. Forget the theatre, study late Dennis Potter, for example, *The Singing Detective*, not *Charley's Aunt. Look at* television, don't just watch it. Listen, analyse, close your eyes and count the words per scene, then look at your own work. Musicians learn music – would you let a blind dentist near your back teeth? All the good writers I know like good writing, they delight in the difficulty of aptness, they are genuinely interested in what words do at nine feet from a domestic screen and at seventy feet from a public stage, etc., etc., etc. You want to do so too – fine – but remember, good intentions have got to be paved with hell.

Starting

Don't start with abstract ideas ('Nobody's done anything about Mixed Bathing For The Unemployed lately . . .'); the best scripts emerge from *situations*, *incidents*, which might or might not eventually illustrate ideas: a grandfather who never talked about Burma until one day he was found gibbering, face downwards, in his tractor – three-foot sheaves were firing at him . . . the French girl you've met who always gets her plurals wrong ('The cat is doing its nuts in the hall') yet who cries every Wednesday evening . . .

These 'seeds' stick because they are not *final*, like a joke or a statement, but cry out for growth, exploration, for example what happens, if just as you are becoming involved and the French girl is about to explain her distress, she disappears? As long as you have researched your subject, and good research is an essential part of the documentary bias of recent television, you will have more to say about the French through character and situation than by abstract statement.

Train yourself to ferret through daily newspapers and your days generally for seeds. Like the disaster at a wedding or a mugging or a forced retirement, those that catch your eye will do so because even if you haven't directly experienced them yourself you can *imagine* them happening to you, or yours, and, again, because what is felt on *your* pulse informs your writing, the situations start to become 'real', 'true'.

If possible talk to the people involved – fact is often richer than fiction. With a good ear, stamina and a wicked need to know, coupled with a growing cultivation of 'experts' you can turn to – your doctor, an indiscreet copper, a lawyer in love with showbiz –suddenly you'll be writing about what you know.

The 'seed', situation or incident won't necessarily mean the opening scene. A girl found quietly setting her friend's bridal gown alight could come at the beginning, in the middle, form the climax, or be the end of a script. Sometimes the seed might even disappear.

Finally, however serious your subject, remember you are in the business of entertainment. Grab your audience in the first minute and don't leave go! This doesn't mean a multiple suicide pact or a car-crash; it can be quiet, witty, chilling, a scene of beauty or a stunning image. The point is – at the start of your tale the audience is the dipper in a bookshop; if the fancy isn't caught the book's put down. Your start is your fingerprint. Your start must have the magic of 'Once upon a time . . .', pushing us to want to know what happens next.

Moving on

Scenes are the building bricks of the script. Whether a scene is a single image, indoors or out, long or short, it will have three components: (i) it has come from somewhere, (ii) it is a stage in the story, and (iii) it moves us on.

A light-hearted example:

Scene 1 A will is being read out to a family on a Saturday morning in the middle of a shopping centre. The provisions produce huge upsets and family members, momentarily reining their anger, depart threatening legal action. The sole beneficiary is a child. One person only congratulates the child – a young woman of twenty. The child smiles with pleasure at her kiss.

The scene abides by all three conditions (having 'grabbed' the audience by the unusual start): (i) it has come from somewhere – someone, obviously with a sense of humour, has died outside the script and that death, or the making of the will, precipitates the drama, (ii) the reading of the will, forming the bulk of the scene, is central to the rest of the story, and (iii) it moves us on – there will be *inevitable* consequences, and what about that single kiss?

Scene 2 The child and his parents are being driven home by the lawyer. Nobody knows what to say. The child smiles unconcerned in the silence. Finally the mother can't help asking if it's all going to be all right. The lawyer smiles . . . enigmatic.

The scene has come from the previous one, the link being the child and the lawyer. The scene is 'about' the dazedness of reaction – dramatic calm after the public brouhaha, and it is physically moving us on by the movement of the car, as well as suggesting doubt for the future through the lawyer's ducking of the question . . .

Scene 3 The girl lets herself into a one-room flat, strangely ill at ease. She doesn't remove her coat but ends up before a large mirror over the mock fireplace. She stares at herself, grins ruefully, removes a ring from the fourth finger of her left hand and places it with delicate precision on the mantelpiece.

A change of angle. In tone her silence matches the dazedness of the child's family in the car. She's come from the first scene, the scene is about her loneliness in a room which might or might not be hers and she pushes the story on with a mysterious gesture.

And we're on our way . . .

As above, scenes can be linked by a person or persons moving physically from one to the next. Scenes can be linked by geography – movement, say, in the same house – and if there is, each room becomes a separate scene. For example:

INTERIOR. LOUNGE. DAY.
Sandra, thirty, prematurely grey, stands
in the middle of the expensive room.
Her eyes show apprehension.

SANDRA Hello?

No reply.

(*Louder.*) Hel-lo?

Silence.
She moves slowly towards the closed
door to the kitchen and
opens it noiselessly.

INTERIOR. KITCHEN. DAY.
She enters –
it is bright, pine-wooded and empty.
Her eyes check everything –
only the larder door is slightly open.
She crosses to it, puzzled,
and pulls it open.

INTERIOR. LARDER. DAY.
The cat hangs by its neck warmly dead.

Scenes can be linked by sound, for example a tune on a car radio is carried on from a spilt Walkman by the side of a sleeping tramp. These are the basic examples of dramatic linkage but what is vital is that scenes move the story on; we are in 'movies', not 'talkies'. Vary the pace, i.e. don't have a necklace of scenes where there's an entrance, something happens and then an exit – that will produce a dead, hump-backed rhythm to your writing. In the tiny example above we start with Sandra already in the room, she doesn't come into it. This forces you to concentrate on her and not the furniture, allows me to have an entry for the next scene and avoids duplication. After Sandra's scream the next scene will probably be elsewhere and involve a red herring with a grin. Vary the length, too, of your scenes and the number of characters in them: a sequence of two-handers can become visually boring, and why deny yourself the *danger* a third character always poses for two, whether gooseberry, intruder, judge or caretaker.

All this might seem obvious but a common fault in starter-writing is to pile event and explanation into the first pages, pell-mell, then have nowhere to go. Tease out the elements of your story and you are drawing on the golden rule of dramatic writing:

DELAY INFORMATION

Delay is the tension of story-telling, whether scene by scene, speech by speech or revelation by revelation. Seek the moment of maximum impact; you don't get climaxes on Page 2. The real intention of the dead man, the enigmatic smile of the lawyer, the girl's gesture, the relationship with the child – and these only in three scenes – are like balloons being floated above the storyline. Never be afraid of throwing these 'balloons' up early on – some will burst but the rest will have to be brought down and used before the end. The more there are, the more options you leave yourself for solving problems of length and twists of the story.

Sometimes, while you're busy avoiding cliché, you'll not be sure why you've left something in – but, just as often, instinct is surer than intent; trust it, you may find a brilliant use for it. But if it's wrong it must go, even if it feels like your blood on the carpet. As long as, at the end of the day, the scenes you have created, the characters you've included and the dialogue you've given them, are all

NECESSARY AND INEVITABLE

you've obeyed the second vital rule. *Anything* superfluous must be cut and better by you than by the winged fowl. A useful tip is to regard a quarter of every page as indulgent: try cutting and sometimes the new leap between two lines (or scenes) can be electric!

One last point on the mechanics of moving the story on.

In my original three scenes, above, concentration on the girl as well as the will has already implied two strands to the story. Most television drama involves double, sometimes triple, even multiple, stranding. One reason for this is that television, being an active rather than a reflective medium, absorbs detail so quickly – images are so final – that it has to be a very strong story to exist singly for an hour or so. A better reason is because double-stranding is so technically useful. While always avoiding a see-saw jumping from one to the other, two strands can thicken and boost the story, gaps in one can be bridged with the other, intertwining can suggest time passing and they allow you to counterpoint mood, or even worlds. At its most obvious it can be seen in a police series episode, the case the copper is investigating is interwoven with domestic problems; at a more sophisticated level, apparently unrelated stories gradually dovetail with unexpected grace. Life is complex and drama should reflect this: double-stranding helps.

Difference

If scenes are the mechanical means of developing your story, difference provides the real drive.

Basic to all drama is the Greek word *agon* meaning 'contest' or 'dispute', both words implying difference. Everyone is different and when differences – of sex, class, age, ambition, job, vocabulary, humour or wealth – meet, *there* is tension and therefore possible drama. Plays are kept going by difference. Your job, as story-teller, is to set up different personalities, let the situations or scenes develop from those differences to provide problems or complications, and then to resolve them. That is the *movement* of a play, not chariot races. Differences can be subtle, shaded, not black and white – in fact a scrap between two people who are both convinced they are right is more dramatic than one right and the other wrong. What is undeniable is that five people sitting around agreeing with each other for two hours is not a play; it may be an inner cabinet but it won't keep the cocoa-drinkers of Ealing up.

Difference, personality, is defined by what your characters *do* and what they *say*. As the conflicts run their course, your characters will change others and be changed. Hardly anyone enters a conflict and emerges unscathed, and part of the pleasure of watching good drama is witnessing the skill with which those changes, those reversals, are brought about.

The tools will be the words you use and the words your characters use. In both cases words are *actions*. Rather like scenes, words come from somewhere, indicate something, and push on the action. Consistent with everything else I've been talking about, they must also be necessary and inevitable.

Stage directions

1.   Never forget you write the *whole* script, not just the dialogue, and stage directions are part of the story you are telling. Therefore they must be as necessary and inevitable as the other elements.

2.   At best they are pure action. Always spell out, on a separate line, each new movement you require – as in the second scene of the Sandra sequence above.

3.   The action should be roughly as long as the time it takes to read the directions slowly. So don't write 'Enter the Red Army; it is wiped out'. Tell us how.

4.   Only include detail you regard as essential. As well as to sets, settings and costume this also applies to character description, for example

Sandra, thirty, prematurely grey

means I intend to do something about that greyness. The rest of Sandra will be revealed through her words and actions.

5.   Never suggest camera shots – the director will do precisely the opposite. Besides, if you start a scene, however brilliant, with *'We open on a long shot of India'*, you have done all writers a bad service.

Dialogue

Writers respect words; like chemicals, words can be made to explode, merely function, or produce sleep. Enjoy them, work hard at aptness, listen and watch; people, after all, wear 'uniforms' in life – a sixty-year-old civil servant does not speak like a docker, a Tesco's shelf-filler or an accident victim. He speaks according to his age, job, sex, humour, class and the demands of the situation you put him in. He will not, except to parody, speak like the others. Dialogue is difference.

It is rarely informational or a rational debate. Seventy-five per cent of the time it's emotional, the nerve ends of feelings – that is why it looks and sounds ungrammatical. People used to each other – say in a marriage or at work – speak shorthand:

> SHE You said we could!
>
>   HE Are we going to have Morecambe all over –
>
> SHE Leave Mum alone! Trust you to –
>
>   HE All right, all right – we've done the milk money – that leaves ten quid! *You tell me how!*

Be very careful when you write dialogue that the *emotional logic* of each character's words is consistent. When one of them changes, or gives in, it will usually be because he or she is emotionally convinced.

But the real problem is that people seldom listen to people; they nod, waiting for the chance to jump in. It has been established that the sense is understood by two-thirds of the way through any sentence – and that is the point when it is cut across and the apparent mayhem above takes place. Yet in its proper context all will make perfect sense!

Pure argument is either medieval or theatrical: you are in television.

Be lucky!

A Good Start?

Michael Wilcox

Your dramatised script, pre-recorded on film or video, is likely to be shown on a small television screen, probably in colour, in someone's living-room. The chances are that the programme will be interrupted by kids, the telephone, visitors, domestic rows, or the family pet demanding attention. The concentration span of the viewer is not aided by factors over which the writer has no control.

Additionally, the remote handset can zap your work. The viewer can flip from channel to channel at the touch of a finger. Assuming that you have survived the commissioning editor, the head of drama, the 'people upstairs', the dreaded script editor, the whims of casting, a director who prefers the work of dead playwrights, the blood on the editing room floor, and the scheduling of your masterwork at a time when all intelligent viewers are in bed, the writer's chances of being seen from beginning to end, without interruption, are small. (Do fifteen million viewers *really* sit in silence for two hours watching *Inspector Morse*?)

Getting your piece off to a good start is essential. You have to capture the attention of the viewer in the opening couple of minutes to escape the 'zap factor'.

The traditional way of starting a drama is to display the title and roll the credits on the star actors. The writer might also get a credit somewhere down the line (the director and producer certainly will!) and all this is accompanied by throat-grabbing music.

(*Action:* Watch the opening sequences of ten dramas on television and make notes on their structure. Include in your survey a couple of soaps, a couple of sit-coms, made-for-television mini-epics, re-runs of cinema movies, and *Screen Two* and *Film on Four* productions.)

If you are writing for a series that has a predetermined style of opening sequences, study the required format carefully and see how it can be exploited to the drama's advantage.

For example, *Inspector Morse* opens with a series of short dramatic sequences that are punctuated by a black screen with titles. Because the black title screens (listing the drama's title, the writer, the star actors, etc.) cut away from one short scene, and then cut back to another, they provide the writer with the opportunity to pack in a great deal of narrative information. The writer can jump from one piece of action, one character, or location, to another, with great freedom. The viewer's attention is captured by so many images, so much narrative action, that the temptation to zap the programme is minimalised.

Here, in the opening sequence of my own *Inspector Morse* episode ('Last Bus to Woodstock'), is what it looks like on the page.

'Last Bus to Woodstock' from *Inspector Morse*

Zenith for Central Television

1   *EXTERIOR. OXFORD ROAD: BUS STOP. NIGHT.*
It is 6.45 p.m. It is dark and starting to rain. Sylvia Kane, in her late teens and fashionably dressed in a yellow raincoat, approaches a bus stop at which an elderly lady, Miss Jarman, is waiting for the bus. Another woman, whose identity we do not see, runs up behind Sylvia. (It is, in fact, Sue Widdowson, a nurse.)

SYLVIA Oh, hello. I'm off to Woodstock. You coming too? Great!

During this Sue responds silently with nods and body language.

Titles.

2   *EXTERIOR. OXFORD ROAD. BUS STOP. NIGHT.*
As the rain falls harder, the two women cover themselves up as best they can. Sylvia has her jacket over her head and Sue has the hood of her anorak up. Sylvia has trotted well ahead of Sue and approaches Miss Jarman.

SYLVIA Excuse, me. When's the next bus, please?
MISS JARMAN Supposed to be here soon. It's generally late.

Titles.

3   *EXTERIOR. OXFORD ROAD. NIGHT.*

Sylvia calls to Sue . . .

SYLVIA Why don't we hitch?

Titles.

4   *INTERIOR. THE FOX AND CASTLE. NIGHT.*
*The public bar of The Fox and Castle pub in Woodstock. It is
getting crowded, even though it is still quite early in the evening.
John Sanders, in his late teens, enters. He looks unsure of himself.
He finds his way to the bar and is about to order when Peter
Newlove, a handsome don, pushes in front of him.*

NEWLOVE Pint of best, please.

Vikki, the barmaid, serves him. John Sanders looks humiliated.

Titles.

5   *EXTERIOR. OXFORD ROAD. NIGHT.*
*A red Ford Escort, driven by a man, (Bernard Crowther), has
stopped to pick up the hitching Sylvia Kane. Sue is some yards
behind Sylvia. The car door opens and Sylvia hops in, shutting her
door. Sue catches sight of the driver, who doesn't see her. The car
drives off, leaving her behind. She turns back to the bus stop and sees
the bus approaching. She joins Miss Jarman, who hardly notices
her, and gets on the bus. Note: The rear nearside lights of the car
are broken.*

Titles.

6   *INTERIOR. THE FOX AND CASTLE. NIGHT.*
*In the bar of The Fox and Castle John Sanders is still on his own, on
a stool at the bar. He is trying to get another pint. He holds up his
empty glass shyly, but Vikki is talking to Peter Newlove. She looks as
though she is being chatted up and is enjoying it. She sees Sanders
and goes over to him.*

VIKKI Same again, love?
SANDERS Yes, please.

She pulls another pint. Newlove leaves the bar.

VIKKI On your own?

SANDERS Supposed to be meeting someone. She's a bit late.

VIKKI Well, it's a pretty nasty night out there.

Vikki gives him the pint and takes his money. Sanders suddenly gets off his stool.

SANDERS Back in a minute!

Titles.

7   *EXTERIOR. THE FOX AND CASTLE. CAR PARK. NIGHT.*

The car park of the pub is packed with cars. We see, from the view-point of someone spying like a peeping tom, that the wondows of a Red Ford Escort are steamed up. There is some action going on inside the car.

Whoever is watching moves closer to see what is going on. Suddenly Sylvia gets out of the car, her clothes in some disarray, and slams the door shut. She looks angry. It is still raining.

Whoever it is that has been watching moves swiftly towards Sylvia and attacks her in a frenzy. Sylvia is beaten to the ground behind the car.

The driver in the car doesn't know what has happened. He has started the car and revved up the engine. He reverses the car violently and drives over Sylvia's neck as she lies on the ground, killing her instantly. The twisted body of Sylvia Kane lies in the rain, lit by the outside lights of the car park.

Note that the scenes are predominantly *visual* rather than *verbal*. This is very important. Viewers use their eyes more than their ears. Visual story-telling grabs the attention. Remember all those domestic distractions! A new programme is starting. Granny wants her cup of tea. The kids are beating hell out of each other. The dog is scraping the paint off the door. With sleight of hand, the writer has to settle the room down again to watch a drama, which will make considerable demands on time and concentration as the complicated plot unfolds. But in the first instance, the opening has to make the viewer think 'What is going to happen next?' or 'That's a bit odd! I don't think she should be doing that!' or 'John Thaw is in this. Let's watch till he comes on the screen.'

By the time John Thaw, as Inspector Morse, does make his first appearance, a girl's body has been discovered in the car park of a public house, the viewer has seen a number of events leading up to her death, has been introduced to possible suspects, and, by the way, has taken in the opening credits. There is also the small matter of the vital clue (the broken rear lights of the car) that has been deliberately planted into the opening seconds of the drama and will not be mentioned again for an hour and a half!

If it is an original, one-off drama (perhaps a *Screen Two* or *Film on Four* film), the writer can construct the opening sequence as he or she wishes. The same principles still apply, as for *Inspector Morse*. The viewer expects to be shown written information about the film on the screen (not in itself all that exciting . . .) and the writer is trying to draw the attention of the viewer into the story.

In the following example, from my *Film on Four* script of *Accounts*, the title information is superimposed on to a succession of dramatic sequences. The viewer *sees* a country funeral, with the two boys and their mother, the moving of the family from one country to another (Northern England to the Scottish Borders) and the vast and wild high fells are established as a major protagonist in the drama from the outset.

Accounts (Film on Four)

SCENE 1. DAY 1, YEAR 1. SEPTEMBER/OCTOBER.
EXTERIOR. THE CHURCHYARD AND SQUARE, ALLENDALE.

Autumn.

The funeral of Harry Mawson is just ending. There is a good crowd, country folk of all ages, dressed in their best, to pay their respects to a well-liked member of the community. Mary Mawson, Harry's widow, perhaps forty, but still a sturdy and attractive woman, and her two sons, Andy and Donald, are the centre of sympathy and attention. Andy is nineteen and Donald seventeen, but the overriding impression one receives from them both, in spite of the well-scrubbed hair and slightly awkward best suits, is of robust health and bursting strength. As the mourners move out of the graveyard and into the village square, one is aware of James Ridley-Bowes hovering attentively a pace or two behind Mary and her sons.

While various villagers approach Mary and the boys to offer sympathy, **the credits start. Music.**

Scene 2. Day 2, Year 1. September/October.
Exterior. Dean Burn farmhouse.

High on the hill overlooking the Allendale Valley and the village.

Credits continue over.

A large red removal van stands outside. The loading is complete. Mary comes out of the house, locking the door for the last time, and hands her keys to James. As the removal van starts to move off down the drive, Mary and the boys climb into the Land-Rover. As they crawl away from the house in the path of the removal van, James is left standing alone beside his little sports car. Then he too gets into his car and drives off. The sheep, Swaledales, graze on unconcerned.

Scene 3. Day 2, Year 1. September/October.
Exterior. Village/open country.

Credits continue over.

The removal van comes down the bank from the farm and into the village. It looks dangerously too big for such a steep and winding lane. In the village it turns right and heads away up a hill and into the open country.

The Land-Rover with Mary and the boys follows it. On reaching the bottom of the bank, James's car turns in the opposite direction, heading for some other undisclosed destination of its own.

Scene 4. Day 2, Year 1. September/October.
Exterior. Northumberland hills.

Titles continue over.

Very wide shot of the rolling Northumberland hills leading towards the Scottish border. The red removal van and the Land-Rover, tiny dots moving along the thin black ribbon which is the road to Scotland.

SCENE 5. DAY 2, YEAR 1. SEPTEMBER/OCTOBER. EXTERIOR. CARTER BAR.

Titles continue over.

The removal van, still followed by the Land-Rover, crosses into Scotland: from this height, the wide expanse of the Scottish Border country is as though laid out before the Mawsons, both daunting and challenging.

SCENE 6. DAY 2, YEAR 1. SEPTEMBER/OCTOBER. EXTERIOR. THE NEW FARM.

The New Farm, an estate agent's 'Sold' notice still in evidence. Here the landscape is different, the hills more rounded, the untamed moorland closer to hand. As the van and the Land-Rover roll up the track towards the farm, **the titles continue over.** *The van stops in the yard. Though well provided with outbuildings, the farm has a slightly unused and forlorn appearance. The boys clamber out of the Land-Rover, followed by Mary. They note the empty house, the rooks nesting in the trees; but any hint of introspection is quickly banished as Mary unlocks the door and the boys move eagerly inside.* **Under the final credits,** *furniture is moved into empty rooms and tea chests of belongings start to be unpacked. We see Mary unwrap a photo of her dead husband, Harry, from an old copy of the 'Hexham Courant' and place it prominently on a mantel.*

Music ends.

You'll see that there is no dialogue at all. The sound accompanying the pictures was carefully constructed. The funeral bell and the shuffling of feet, the sound of the vehicles, the wind, the sheep, an original music score and the odd, unscripted comment as the van was unloaded and the boys shouted at one of the sheep dogs . . . all combined to give the film a spontaneous realism.

After the film was edited, it was decided to over-dub a few comments from Mary Mawson about how her decision to move was made in the belief that it was in the best interests of the boys. We were concerned that the use of purely visual information might make too many demands on the viewer, who (unlike us, of course) had no idea what the story was going to be about. So there *might* be some flexibility available at the editing stage, but remember that you can only be creative with footage that has actually been shot. So the most careful consideration must be given at the scripting and filming stages of the project, rather than depending on adjustments in post-production.

Video or film?

If you are being commissioned to write for a specific series of dramas, you will of course have to consider the technical and logistical resources that are available. How long is the script to run for? Will it be recorded in a studio or on location? Or will it be a combination of each? If so, what proportion can be made on location? Will it be shot on film or video? Your script will have to conform to a whole bunch of predetermined criteria.

Does this sound restricting? It's best to try not to think of it like that. You'll know from the outset what the resources are, and it is part of the job of the writer to exploit all that is available to the fullest extent.

Film and video, to this writer, are different resources. Each has advantages over the other. Video allows for instant replay of the scene just recorded. If anything has gone wrong technically, you can see it there and then. The director can go for another take. Film, on the other hand, has to be sent away to be processed. The whole business of dispatching, processing, returning and viewing 'rushes' is time consuming, expensive and, on some locations, infuriatingly complicated.

Until *Film on Four* broke the mould of British television drama by using film exclusively, the writer was generally writing for studio-based, videotaped productions. Much of the editing was done during the actual performance, switching between one camera and another. From the writer's point of view, this technique was likely to demand a dialogue-based script, rather than a series of visuals. Television studio drama seemed only one step away from traditional theatre writing. As a consequence, experienced theatre writers were able to find a second home for their skills, and a source of income to supplement the tiny amounts of money usually available from theatrical work.

As a result of years of studio-based television drama, British writers seem to have concentrated their skills on writing dialogue at the expense of developing their visual imaginations. Maybe that generalisation is being grossly unfair to some writers. Nevertheless, in my own experience, producers, script readers, directors and technicians too often show a limited visual imagination. Their approach to drama is too literary and verbal.

I still burn with fury at one director who, at the read-through of a half-hour studio-based video drama, told the assembled company: 'Don't bother with the stage directions. We'll just read the dialogue!' We started our read-through on page six of my script! When I protested, I was told not to interrupt.

Without wishing to make rules, a writer might conclude that a studio-based video drama is likely to be dominated by theatrical diaogue; a drama recorded on location with hand-held or tripod-mounted video cameras allows for far greater visual flexibility, at the expense of pure dialogue; and a filmed drama is likely to be the most purely visual of all. This is, of course, an over-simplification. Independent directors and pop-video specialists have shown what a wonderful visual medium video can be. The problem for writers is that directors of such originality tend to work outside television and not within it.

(*Action:* Watch ten different television dramas and note whether they are video based in the studio or on location, or filmed dramas. Compare the visual qualities of each and note the ratio of dialogue scenes to purely visual scenes. Decide how successful the production has been in exploiting the technical potential of the medium adopted.)

Here, finally, is the opening of *Midnight Feast*, a thirty-minute, studio-based video drama. It is set in a boys' boarding school in Scotland. Although the script is dialogue based on a single set, I have tried to create movement and visual story-telling as part of the drama. In doing this, I have tried to exploit the filmic potential of a single set.

A 'single set' does not necessarily mean that all the action occurs in one room. Even a small television studio allows for the possibility of various locations to be incorporated in the small space available. In *Midnight Feast* (an STV production), the main action occurred in the housemaster's study, but we also saw his kitchen, hallway and a corridor, which, from the design point of view, constituted part of the 'single set'.

Midnight Feast (STV *Preview* series)

1   *INTERIOR. HALLWAY. 11.30 P.M.*

Two boys, Stevens and Straun, enter from the boys' side through a frosted panelled door. They wear dressing gowns and carry torches. The hall light is already on.

They creep into the hallway and make for the study door, which is closed.

2   *INTERIOR. STUDY.*

The door opens. No light on in the study. Torches of the two boys as they enter.

Straun checks that the curtains are securely drawn.

Stevens turns on the lamp, which stands on the housemaster's desk. He places half a bottle of whisky in the middle of the desk.

Straun searches inside a cabinet, and produces two cut-glass tumblers. He sets them down beside the half-bottle of whisky.

Stevens sits himself down in the housemaster's chair behind the desk.

Straun finds himself a wooden chair, places it in front of the desk and sits down on it.

Stevens pours out two measures of whisky. He slides a glass across the desk top to Straun.

They raise their glasses and drink simultaneously.

Straun tosses his glass over his shoulder.

Unintentionally, it smashes through a glass-fronted bookcase.

STRAUN Christ!

Stevens turns out the light. Has anyone heard them? They turn on their torches.

Straun goes to the door. Opens it.

3   *INTERIOR. HALLWAY.*

Straun peers out into the hallway.

Quiet.

The sound of a distant flushing lavatory on the boys' side.

4   *INTERIOR. STUDY.*

Straun closes the door again.

Stevens turns the lamp back on again.

STEVENS You're mad, Straun.

Straun fetches another glass. Then he takes out a third glass.

STRAUN I'm going to fetch some ice.

Straun goes to the door.

5   *INTERIOR. HALLWAY.*

Straun crosses the hallway to the kitchen. He opens the kitchen door.

6   *INTERIOR. KITCHEN.*

Straun turns the light on.

He goes to the fridge, opens it and gets out the ice box. He tries to lever the ice cubes from it, and suddenly it flies on to the floor and ice cubes scatter everywhere.

7   *INTERIOR. STUDY.*

Stevens is exploring.

He goes to the bookcase with the smashed glass front and tries to tidy things up. He notices something behind a row of books. He takes some books out and discovers a box of After Eight Mints.

8   *INTERIOR. KITCHEN.*

Straun is loading up with ice cubes.

He checks out the fridge, but there is nothing much in it. He checks out other cupboards in the kitchen, but there is a surprising lack of food.

9   *INTERIOR. STUDY.*

Stevens is searching in drawers, behind books, in the corner cupboard. He is discovering all sorts of delightful delicatessen foods hidden away, much to his astonishment.

Tatty's hidden delicatessen supplies include: pâté, smoked ham (fresh and thinly cut), all the ingredients needed for a freshly tossed salad (including the salad bowl and wooden utensils), herring mops, and a store of different types of biscuits. All these items are hidden, ingeniously, in the study. It may be that there are other hiding places, with secret stores, that the boys fail to discover.

Stevens is starting to load up the desk top with an interesting spread.

Straun returns with the ice cubes.

STRAUN My God, Stevens!
STEVENS Check out that chest, Straun.

Stevens discovers a cheese board in the bottom drawer of the desk.

STEVENS What a stink! Doesn't look too bad.

Straun opens a chest and takes out some games equipment . . . bats, pads, stumps . . . then he discovers bananas, oranges, grapes . . . which he takes over to the desk. There is now a splendid collection of food.

STEVENS The secret life of Tatty Tay!

Now compare this with the opening sequence of *Accounts*, the *Film on Four* production. In each case, the viewer is led into the story visually, rather than verbally. Even working on a tiny budget in a small space in *Midnight Feast*, the amount of detail required of the designer and the complexity of movement and intimate camera work that the script demands, show that small and cheap does *not* mean a lack of ambition on the part of the writer. Indeed, to challenge the technical and artistic resources of all those involved in the production, in a fair and realistic manner, is one way of getting the best out of everybody.

Structuring Your Story

Iain Heggie

When I first started writing I think I thought that structure was for critics. Audiences and writers didn't bother with it. A play was its details. Then when my work began to be performed it couldn't escape my notice that the audience seemed to reserve its biggest responses for all those aspects of my work which I could only describe as structural. The things I had written anyway, without trying. This made me want to understand these aspects better and use my discoveries. When I began to explore 'structure' in my own way and to translate what I found into my own words I found it not only helpful but positively stimulating. It is the purpose of this chapter to try and share some of this stimulus.

Up till now I have written for the theatre. However, the kinds of structural concerns which are discussed here are relevant to drama in all the media: radio, theatre, cinema and television.

Too many commentators have told me that British writers are hostile to thinking about structure for it to have no truth. The word 'structure' seems to imply fitting into rather than being liberated by a pre-existing set of rules, suppressing rather than expressing what you really have to say. And that if you do take an interest in it you run the risk of letting 'form' ride roughshod over 'content'. In my own case, the only way that I came into contact with 'structure' was either *unconsciously* in the experience of a play or when a critic would write that the structure was too this or too that. Almost too unspecific, in other words, for my needs as a writer *or* to reflect my experience as an audience.

The audience made me realise that I had written structurally. Every time I went away from what the audience experienced the structure to be, the quality of their attention reduced. At such times they tended to wait patiently (or not so patiently) for their idea of the structure to begin. An audience being patient or impatient with me is not my idea of heaven. It was all too haphazard, the audience's attention level couldn't be left to chance. I would have to take what they gave to the event – their time – into account. What you structure when you write a play is, I believe, primarily the time of the audience. I would have to start trying to tally what I want the audience to attend to with the amount of time I was expecting them to give up to it. The writer may well only *share* control of what the audience see and hear with the actors, designer and director, but when it comes to the over-all shape of the time dimension in a play or film the writer has almost exclusive control.

The active question

The audience responds when you ask them to look forward in time, to expect. Then the audience responds again when you deliver their expectations. But the audience responds particularly well when their expectations are *exceeded*. We introduce the audience to character A, who makes us look forward to a meeting with character B. Before the meeting we receive other information which pertains to the meeting, makes us expect, but does not tell us precisely what will happen. In the event the combination of A and B and all the circumstances gives us all that is predicted; but if *the combination* gives, in the event, much more, then the audience is involved, excited and surprised. In a word, heightened, and most ready to receive at such times what a playwright most wants to say.

How can you make the audience expect? I think audiences give their best attention when the writer unlocks their wish to put their desires into action. Not necessarily to 'approve' or deem such a desire wise, but certainly to experience a direct connection to it. The playwright's task is to set up circumstances which make the enactment of the desire necessary. Someone has to want something badly. In terms of the world of the play it has to be a feasible desire – problematic, but feasible. If it is made necessary to embark on the enactment of a desire in a context which makes it both feasible and problematical, the audience will begin to expect, their attention will begin to heighten. And if during the course of putting that desire into action the audience is asked to spend too much time attending to unrelated things the quality of their attention declines. The desire has to be compelling enough to ensure that it will result in action, which will take *time*. The audience loses interest if it is impossible to proceed with the desire in *all* its aspects.

The best way I have found to formulate the desire is in the form of a question. The question does not include the conditions and circumstances which make the desire both feasible and problematical. The question asks what the task is, but does not describe it. It does not necessarily show you how to interpret the play. Rather, by uniting the audience's attention by making them look forward to the answering of the question it unites the audience's time. The play is over when the question is as answered as it can be. In *Hamlet* – should mother re-marry? or is there really something rotten in Denmark? are not active questions. However much Shakespeare might desire the play to make us speculate about these issues, the questions lead to thought, rather than action. The active question in *Hamlet* is 'How can I kill my stepfather?'. In *Macbeth* it is 'How can I become King and stay King?. In Scorsese's *After Hours* it is 'How can I escape from this environment?'. In his *King of Comedy* it is 'How can I do my comedy act on live television?'.

The active question differs from the specific objectives of a character within a scene because it tends to structure a whole play. The question is being asked near the beginning and the consequences of the resulting action are fully realised by the end.

In David Mamet's *Edmond* the question is 'How can I leave my old life behind and come alive?'. As part of that, in one scene, Edmond's objective is to achieve some kind of sexual gratification with a prostitute.

I believe that it is a useful exercise to try to construct an active question which you think would lead to a play. One way into this would be to explore a desire which you turned away from for one reason or another.

I go swimming in my local pool. Because I often feel hungry after swimming and I want to avoid eating the junk on sale at the pool I often take fresh fruit with me to eat on the way home. One day, after swimming, I got dried and dressed. I wanted to attend to my hair in another part of the changing area. It would only take a minute, so, making sure I had my wallet in my pocket, I decided to risk leaving my kit complete with banana beside the locker I had used. I was gone less than a minute, but sure enough, when I came back the banana had gone. I knew instantly that there was nothing I could do. All practical attempts to recover the banana would lead me to some kind of embarrassment. I left without it. But it occurred to me that if I had given the problem to a character who was less vulnerable to embarrassment or who was willing to be embarrassed or who would be unable to predict the embarrassment, the active question would be 'How do I get my banana back?'. If anyone finds this too trivial to be worthy of sustained interest my thought is that either it would make a short play or that the trivial question could be made to illustrate serious themes, as in *Citizen Kane* 'How do I discover the significance of Rosebud?'.

The size of the active question: the length of the play

If I am right in assuming that a play of a film is most effectively structured by the active question, then the length of the piece should be dictated by how long the audience is willing to pursue the answer. Some active questions are more worthy of pursuit at length than others. In general, my guess is that 'How do I become and stay King?' has more potential for lengthy treatment than 'How do I get my banana back?'. The desire for absolute power has many contexts in which it could be fascinating at length, whereas the desire for one of the world's many bananas has few.

The theme and the active question

The way that I understand the old idea that drama is dreaming in public is that it is at its most compelling when it releases desires which we normally suppress. Desires which, for whatever reason, can only be achieved by breaking the law, cheating, betraying, behaving antisocially or working against your own nature, skills or beliefs. As in *Macbeth*, *Hamlet*, *King of Comedy* and *Edmond*. In framing an active question fit to span the time given by the audience I try to ensure that the goal cannot be achieved by the application of common sense or good citizenship. On one hand, the active question must demand a response; on the other, it must be sufficiently difficult not to be answered simply. While it is true that the active question must be responded to, the most compelling questions are those which have no perfect answer. Those where the question is answered at great cost or where the cost is foreseen and, in practice, prevents the answering of the question. In Shakespearean tragedy the question is answered but the central character pays for the resulting action with his life. In Chekhov lack of skill to see a plan of action through or lack of willingness to risk failure makes the characters keep failing at the first hurdle. Examples of active questions framed precisely to stress the element of impossibility would be 'How do I kill my landlady and live a normal life afterwards?' or 'How do I tell someone I love them without *any* risk of embarrassment or rejection?'.

Who asks the active question?

In Shakespeare and in many modern American films the question is asked on our behalf through one or two central characters. In successful drama I think the choice of character itself should illustrate aspects of the difficulty of the active question: in *Hamlet*, for example, 'How can I kill my stepfather?' is given to a man who is slow to action and inclined to reflections which make him able to predict unpleasant consequences.

In Chekhov *all the characters* tend to have a stake in closely related active questions. In David Mamet's play *Glengarry Glen Ross* the characters ask 'How best to survive?' around the selling of real estate.

Character and the active question

If the writer creates his or her character from those aspects of humanity which best illustrate the difficulty of the active question, the result should be that the character cannot refuse to act. Characters are not human beings. They are constructed to go into action. To go into action urgently enough, that is, to make the play or film really begin to move soon after the arrival of the audience.

Subdivisions of the active question

Time in many plays and films is subdivided into acts and scenes. This breaking up of the audience's time is a way of maintaining the audience's attention. A play cannot be one preparation phase and one delivery phase. Rather there are lots of preparations and lots of deliveries. In effect each preparation and delivery is the setting up and the enactment of a task which – it is anticipated – will eventually lead to the answering of the active question.

In the first act of *Othello*, Iago achieves the first part of his plan, to come between Desdemona's father and Othello and therefore get Roderigo on his side. The act ends not only with completion, Iago on a high point, it also prepares for more to come: sketched-in plans to come between Othello and Cassio. A plan which we know from earlier in the act must involve some outrageous action. We anticipate.

The world of the play and the active question

The writer can focus the attention of the audience harder on the active question by creating an imaginative world in which the outrageous journey to the answering of the question is both heightened and made likely. Shakespeare gives Hamlet a world full of practical, eager and vulgar characters to set off the dilemmas of his intellectuality. This world on the one hand keeps renewing his need to see his aims through and on the other effortlessly thwarts it.

In *After Hours* the camera is a useful tool in creating the film's world. Through the camera we often see with the protagonist: we see *what* and *how* he sees. When he has accepted the hospitality of the girl and goes back to her flat, he sees something in a bag which arrests his attention. It suggests he has reasons to be frightened of the girl. The camera latches on to the object as though it is obsessed. In an instant we have apprehended a new and complex obstacle. How does the protagonist get what he wants from the girl *or* escape without endangering himself? Simultaneously we recognise the difficulty the character has with his tendency to find things to be scared of.

Types of shots and an imaginative use of the camera is a very important device in helping to create a world for the screen.

Time and the active question

Time is a very useful way to bring the active question into focus because it can make situations urgent. It acts as a pressure on characters against delay. It helps to make the play happen soon after the arrival of the audience.

In *Macbeth*, the visit of Duncan for a *limited duration* must be taken advantage of. His departure acts as a kind of deadline which ends the best opportunity for action.

In *The King of Comedy* the central character kidnaps a television host to enable himself to get a live appearance as a stand-up comic. When the programme controllers agree he leaves the kidnap victim with his sidekick. The kidnap victim manages to escape and this creates tension about whether there will be time for him to stop the broadcast. Of all American films the central character in this film is the most startlingly unlovable; nevertheless there is no doubt that the film makes you look forward through this tension in a mixture of hope and dread. You look forward to the realisation of his (and our?) moment of fame.

Location and the active question

Location in drama is at its best when it heightens the action. Too often the location in theatre and television is chosen because that is the place where it *would* happen. This is pedantry. It disburdens the writer of the need to choose and to create location. The audience is loaded with an unnecessary encumbrance: irrelevant or merely observant location.

Shakespeare locates Duncan's bedroom off stage so that Lady Macbeth has to wait for Macbeth's return. We worry and imagine. He comes back covered in blood with the daggers in his hands, out of control. Lady Macbeth fails to calm him down and has to return the daggers herself. When someone starts to knock at another door, Macbeth's hysterics increase. The precise locating of the action in this scene forces the audience to wait, to imagine, to fear. Had we been in that room with him in the theatre the mechanics of the actual killing could have reduced our experience of the consequences of the action and what new action it must lead to.

In *Rear Window*, Hitchcock traps his injured central character in a room with a view round the back of an enclosed block of flats. The central character discovers and solves the mystery by piecing together clues from events glimpsed through people's windows.

Macbeth uses location theatrically, *Rear Window* uses it cinematically to heighten and colour the process of answering the active question.

Revelation and the active question

Most drama must give the audience the information it needs early in the timespan of the action. The time when the audience is most willing to receive it. However, a piece of well-timed information or a revelation well into the action can throw a new obstacle in the way of the active question.

In *A Streetcar Named Desire*, when Stanley Kowalski hears rumours about Blanche Dubois, he betrays her to the man she had some hopes of marrying. In fact, Blanche never recovers from this setback and the desire she wishes to activate – 'How can I find a safe home?' – flops and falters. This revelation shapes the active question process in the play by beginning the downward movement, the failure to come up with the answer. The audience begins to predict this. We continue to pay attention to see *how* Blanche will fail.

Secondary characters and the active question

In most drama the biggest obstacles and opportunities to the answering of the active question come from the other characters. Lady Macbeth encompasses Macbeth's state of mind and helps him with the practical difficulties. She is an opportunity in the sense that she is the prime activator of Macbeth's desire. In *Edmond*, practically all the disillusionment and frustrations of the central character's desire stem from other characters, who are more grossly opportunist, more vulgarly romantic or more mundanely pragmatic than suits him. Certainly in a central character-led play or film you could see secondary characters as phased illustrations of different aspects of the answering of the active question.

The active question as a tool for writing

As a working writer I cannot afford to wait till I become an expert play-wright before I write my next play. The only use for reading about writing is if it helps you do what you want to do. The idea of the active question has stimulated recent work of mine. Particularly in relation to over-all structure, how long things should last, where in the play things should be and relevance to the action. I don't believe it should be used reverently. And I am sure that for many people, including me, to understand playwriting perfectly before you start to write would kill the desire to write.

Note from Editors: Scorsese's work is widely available on video; David Mamet's plays, like Shakespeare and Chekhov, are available in published form for further study.

The Breath of Inspiration

Stephen Lowe

For years I banged my head against the proverbial and sometimes literal brick wall, waiting on inspiration. On the days it didn't visit, I fell into drink, and despair. And, as I had read of suffering for one's art, I foolishly convinced myself this torture was all part of the creative process. I understood only one meaning of inspiration:

> INSPIRATION noun.
> 1. Divine influence, esp. that which is thought to prompt poets.

When it didn't 'prompt' me, I 'died' like an actor on stage who has 'dried'. The problem was that that definition gave me no clue as to how to find my way to the 'divine influence'. The other definition, however, did:

> INSPIRATION noun.
> 1. Drawing in of breath.

Much simpler. In fact, it couldn't be much clearer:

1. Inspiration is that which gives us life itself, that breathes life into us.

2. Without it we are dead. An indispensable human activity.

3. I am not dead. Therefore, I am inspiring.

4.   But I am as clearly conscious of the process going on as, normally, I am about my breathing.

5.   I simply have to become conscious of what is already going on inside me.

I admit to being slow. It took me six years to understand that I, like everyone else, am already inspiring. I simply needed to become aware of it, and eliminate anything that blocked or limited it.

The writer's block

Inspiration is the intake of breath, not its expiration. But is dependent on it. If we don't breathe out, then no air can come in, and we die. The manner in which we breathe out, the depths to which we clear our lungs, the tensions we impose on our chest and back – all these control whether the inspiration is shallow and restricted or full and rich. It is pointless trying to work on the inspired breath directly – you can't squeeze any more air into the lungs than you have expired. As an actor, attempting to gain 'voice control', I foolishly worked on the intake, trying to choke more down, gasping at the air, until an excellent voice coach explained the misdirection of my efforts. However, we can assist the clearing of the lungs, the expiration, to create the vacuum for inspiration to occur more freely. Stanislavski's and other acting techniques have extended this notion of clearing the ground not only to the body, but to the feelings and thoughts of an actor. It is part of becoming 'receptive', as opposed to 'blocked'. It is attention and focus (rather than tension and discipline). It is also extremely hard work. As a playwright you have to prepare your own arena. Peter Brook calls a similar meeting ground in the theatre the empty space. Having done this, then you sit back and wait. You can, for the moment, do little else.

In my experience, when it comes, inspiration is often in the shape of a living image, brief, fragile, but itself breathing, and this image is the fusion of both form and content. Prior to this moment, there may have been months of entertaining thoughts on a certain subject, deep research, interviews, essays, but the moment it becomes alive, animated, is when something takes hold and creates an image.

Art is ruled uniquely by the imagination. Images are its only wealth. It does not classify objects, it does not pronounce them real or imaginary, does not qualify them, does not define them; it feels and presents them – nothing more.

(Benedetto Croce, *Aesthetic*)

Just as we are all inspiring, so are we all image-makers.

However, apart from within a few privileged areas, image-making is a much-derided attribute in contemporary society. Every night our dreams are full of images, and they lie there scarcely buried under the surface of our so-called consciousness as we work during the day. But we are told to push them away, not to daydream, not to dwell on things, snap out of it – in short, to pay attention to some other reality dictated by another.

The playwright, as an act of perversity, decides to do the opposite, believing that these images are perhaps not mere distraction, or escapism, but may hold a key to some deeper truth, or simply that they are more fun, more alive, than the specific task in hand.

What are the images a playwright works with?

This is the first paradox of an activity surrounded by paradox. As I've already revealed by my total lack of interest in 'literary style', I am not a writer. I am a playwright. I am not involved in a literary pursuit. I make, I 'wright', not write. For a clear description of the implications of this essential distinction I'd recommend you study John Arden's superb essay on playwrighting in his *Pretend the Pretense* – that alone might save you much confusion. So, like a shipwright, a cartwright, I 'make' plays. And here is another paradox.

Worker's playtime

The word 'wright' carries with it the notion of work, and 'play' is per-ceived in our society as its opposite. So be it. I work and play at the same time. But so strong is the Calvinist work ethic in us that we often daren't allow ourselves enough space to play. Embarrassed by the childish nature of our activity, we become intent (and intense) on demonstrat-ing our seriousness, and the 'validity' of our noble craft. In doing so, we all too often kill its very strength, we literally throw out the splashing, playing baby and the plastic duck with the bath-water. We end up with earnest, well-covered, extremely meaningful, and totally lifeless plays. The baby or the plastic duck could both have told us there is nothing more boring than earnest, well-covered, extremely meaningful, and totally lifeless plays. You have to splash a little or there is no point in being in the bath.

So don't forget to play. Don't feel guilty. Have some fun. The work is clearing the ground, the play is – whatever, whoever enters it.

You've paid for your ticket. Now take your seat

But don't expect the mind simply to go blank, any more than the lungs will stop breathing. What happens is that this 'clearing away' reveals deeper desires, and yearnings. It is accompanied by a shift from the des-perate desire to control and manipulate, to a point where I slowly become not the active maker of images, but the audience hopefully wait-ing for 'something to happen', yearning for some as yet unknown image to fulfil some perhaps equally unknown, unarticulated need. I become the best, the most demanding, the most alive audience I can. I won't be fobbed off with a bad game. As images arrive, I reject and accept them just as children take up, transform or drop games as their inner need dic-tates. Audiences watch and are connected with the plays and games we offer them according to these inner needs. It is this as yet inarticulate and unexpressed desire, however, that shapes the game.

We know that even God could not imagine the redness of a
red Geranium
nor the smell of mignonette
when geraniums were not, and mignonettes neither . . .
But imagine, among the mud and the mastodons
God sighing and yearning with tremendous creative yearn-
                            ing, in that dark green moss
Oh, for some other beauty, some other beauty
that blossomed at last, red geranium, and mignonette.

                            (D. H. Lawrence)

Les règles de jeu

God, of course, has rather a lot of resources at his disposal. His inspiration can take practically any form. The point is, it has to take a certain
form, it has to breathe life into a certain frame. My experience, both as
an ex-literary manager and from workshopping with playwrights both
here and abroad, is that most do not pay sufficient attention to the
potentials, and distinctions, of the various playwrighting forms themselves. They regard such considerations as restrictive, rather than seeing
the apparent rules of a form as capable of offering inspirational ideas. All
too often, the inexperienced playwright seems to think a 'divine' idea
appears, and then it can simply be translated into whichever form is
most available. In my experience, this is the opposite of the truth. The
moment of inspiration is when form and content merge. A major part of
my work is to consider the medium itself, and a major part of my play is
concerned with the medium itself.

As ideas and the first tentative images come to me, I imaginatively
explore them via the possibilities of differing media. But, in order to be
able to play like this, it's essential I have a strong sense of the way images
operate in the different 'play' media (the theatre itself with a myriad of
different presentational forms, film, television, radio) – I move
imaginatively around the image as a camera; or relate to it in the specific
confines of the theatre audience; I listen to the sounds of it closing off
all visual images. Each will reveal a new facet, a new possibility.

It is not that each medium simply offers a different way to say the
same thing. Having over the past ten years turned my stage play *Touched*,

about women in Nottingham at the end of the Second World War, into a radio play, and now into a script for a television film, I am very conscious of how impossible such a thing is. That is not a disappointment. Each new language offers the possibility to say something different, to reach into areas the other media could not reach (while of course losing what they were strong in). Because of this the work becomes alive again.

Each so-called translation should be a celebration

of the new medium

More than half the plays I see in workshops are ideas uncertain of their home, and, as such, often very good ideas fail to inhabit the correct medium to engage its audience. All too often a stage play is really masquerading unhappily as a radio play, the radio play seems to think the viewer can see what is not communicated by language and sound, the television script struggles with the epic sweep of the film, the film is locked in some mid-distance shot as though it were a stage play being seen from the same seat in the centre of the third row back. Such a state of affairs is a failure of the imagination. It is failed image-making. And I suspect one of the reasons for it is a fear about the intricacies of the differing languages themselves.

Don't be afraid.

If you look at the various media for the virtues of their image-making process, it can become a liberation to your work/play. You don't need any secret knowledge to discover this. It is, however, of primary importance to experience the medium as one of the audience. This sounds so obvious as to be embarrassing, but if I had a pound for every radio play submitted by people who have spent months writing in and never bothered to listen in to the afternoon play I could retire. The number of sit-coms written by people who have clearly never seen one would take your breath away. So –

Open up. Let us others inspire you. Be willing to learn. If only not to repeat their mistakes. It is a disastrous combination of arrogance and stupidity to think you have nothing to learn from the work of others.

Of course, with television everyone thinks they know it. Haven't we all spent our lives watching it? Couldn't we all do better?

Probably. So what stops us? Well, many feel that, while being expert 'audiences' with stories to tell, there is some arcane technical language – that of the mystery of the cameras – that prevents them from 'writing for the box'. There is no mystery of the camera as far as I'm concerned.

The mystery of the camera revealed

1.   It can operate any distance away from its object, as long as the front of it is pointed towards it.

2.   It can move towards it/away from it/around it/along with it.

3.   It can cut to something else.

To a playwright having a medium like that is totally inspiring. Look over an image you are playing with, with this eye.

And look at the television set itself, from the perspective of seeing its form not as restrictive, but as a liberation.

The television screen was created as a box to contain the image of a human head. This head could educate us with the news, lecture or sermon, or entertain us with a song or a joke, but it would largely talk directly to, or at, us. The head was intended to be perceived as roughly life size from the viewing distance of some six feet away. I've always felt television sets should not be placed on stands (making everybody look like Evil Edna in *Will of the Wisp*) but should rest on the shoulders of a dummy you sat in the armchair in the corner. But the whole head has to be shown. If you use extreme close-ups, sectionalising the face, giant mouths, eyes, something unnerving happens to the viewer in a way that wouldn't in the cinema. Cinema's unnatural size encourages in the viewer a different aesthetic acceptance of an already sectionalised, partial, and enlarged world.

Even with a twenty-six-inch television, the most successful moments are still two people, side by side, talking directly to us (there is simply not enough space to allow them realistically – i.e. at a life-size level – to talk to each other). Note here the distinction between the Two Ronnies comfortably talking to us as comic newsreaders, and the strangely intimate and rather disturbing Smith and Jones whispering to each other in profile.

These heads are the magnetic centre of television: its mainstay is either a face staring out at us, or two faces being pulled closer and closer together. Everything else is a dance around that. This became the inspiration for my recent *Screen Two* film, *Ice Dance*, when I heard Christopher Dean, the Olympic skater, say the world had never seen the major 'transformation' moments in their performance, as these were facial expressions that only the judges could witness (cameras being barred from being placed behind the judges). I wanted to see the moments I was barred from seeing. I wanted the mobility the camera had, to track and follow these dances, to move away from them so the whole pattern could be seen and to cut back to close-up to see the expression of the dancers' faces. It was from this, from images of the two dancers' separate faces, and the magnetic pull to bring those faces together, that the whole piece was shaped. That was the visceral tension in the viewer that I was exploring. It clearly could not have worked half so well on stage, or as a radio piece. Inspired by the potential of the form, I was sustained through the months of research, playmaking and filming.

Exploring the apparently intimate life-size nature of television has always fascinated me, from my first *Play For Today*, *Cries From a Watchtower*, in 1979. There I wanted to explore the implications of the then little-discussed silicon chip technology on the life of an ordinary man, and I chose a watchmaker. The 'tension' lay between his growing awareness of the enormity of the problem he was encountering, and his diminishing control over the carefully organised components of the mechanical watch. The camera could move from the minutiae of the watch to his face and on to the wider world. But his face, his emotional life, lay at the heart of it. This the television camera can well explore, since television operates, at least semi-consciously, on this line. It can be explored, transformed and challenged. That is one of the interesting games.

Another example is playing with perspectives. After all, the television screen is flat. It simply works hard to deceive us it's otherwise. In 1985 I adapted a stage play of mine, *Kisses on the Bottom*, for BBC2. Its characters were those on seaside postcards – Fat Mum, Henpecked Husband, Honeymoon Couple, Jock the Scot, the Vicar . . . Originally directed for the stage by Alan Ayckbourn, it had never occurred to me it could make a television play. But the director argued it could work simply because it cut across the commonly held misconceptions of television. We would flatten out the image, make the whole piece within the flat, shadowless world of the postcards.

There are many other examples. The key point is, look at the medium, and let its potential inspire you; let it fuse and play with your other concerns and images. Do not wright for a medium that does not inspire you. If you do, you will fail to inspire it. And as playwrighting is part of a collective artistic activity involving not only your creativity but that of many others such a state would not augur well for success.

'T-T-T-Timing'

Paul Jackson

The view that in comparison to the serious drama, comedy is a secondary art, a lightweight diversion, has long pervaded our theatrical and television industries. How often has it been said of a serious classical actor, 'He's quite good at light comedy too, you know', with all the dismissive undertones of someone pointing out that Viv Richards could bowl a bit, if pressed? Far too many people working full time in our business who really should know better, consider comedy to be the nursery slopes or the rest and recuperation zone before the serious business of the drama.

This attitude flies in the face of two simple truths: firstly, comedy is and always has been the art which engages the widest and most loyal audience. The ability to laugh at the world around us, to mock our own sufferings, to make light of our difficulties, to puncture pomposity or authority, to ridicule evil or aggression, is at the centre of our social mechanisms. Secondly, the writers, performers, directors or producers of comedy – indeed anyone involved with the making of a comic performance – face exactly the same range of challenges as their dramatic colleagues. They have to develop a plot-line, portray certain characters, engage the audience emotionally and intellectually, they have to time their work against the audience's anticipated reaction as they rehearse and then against the actual reception of a performance. They have to communicate and manipulate with equal subtlety and with equal conviction. Both schools ultimately demand the suspension of disbelief, but don't let anyone tell you that comic characters don't have to bother with establishing themselves realistically, that a quick stereotyped caricature will do for farce. In truth nothing is more guaranteed to kill a laugh dead than a superficial, unrealistic performance. Comedy is rooted in truth; the recognition laugh when an audience effectively says, yes, I've been in that situation or I've known that person, is one of the trade's most valued techniques.

Anyone engaged in the creation of comedy has to wrestle with all these difficulties of straightforward dramatic work but with one massive layer of complexity added on – the laughter itself.

Let us take just one specific example, the writer. The successful writer of any dramatic script needs to be in control of a variety of factors to make the piece work and if they are not there a producer's response is likely to feature all those only too familiar phrases: 'The plot does not work.' 'The characters do not develop.' 'The rhythm is wrong.' Perhaps I can try to explain what is usually intended by these notes.

The plot-line

Television comedy, working as it so often does in runs of half-hour chunks, has sometimes tended to see plot as a time-consuming luxury. Disappointingly often, the plot of an average sit-com consists of no more than the introduction of a single unexplained catalyst into the pre-established order of the series situation with the intention of setting the central characters running around aimlessly for twenty-five minutes (say twenty-one on ITV) until an equally unexplained resolution materialises. It is worth noting, however, how many of the accepted classics of the genre have in fact relied heavily on careful plot development.

John Cleese's dedication to clarity of structure is legendary; certainly his twelve *Fawlty Towers* scripts all demonstrate the most meticulous attention to detail as each episode starts with the desperate attempt at normality before the inevitable descent through an increasing barrage of adversity into the depths of chaos and confusion.

The Hancock scripts constantly evolve and then resolve (think of the classic pay-off to the Blood-Donor script), a technique which Galton and Simpson persisted with in *Steptoe and Son*. Virtually any episode of *Taxi* or *Cheers* will set up and resolve a specific incident, often taking in detailed sub-plots as well, all in the space of twenty-four minutes. *The Young Ones* made a feature of inventing a ludicrous plot and then treating it with complete disregard, and of course serious drama has consistently experimented with the anti-plot or the plotless play (Beckett and Ionesco spring immediately to mind) but such scripts still need a rhythm of events to move them forward and this rhythm will need to be orchestrated.

I personally am always suspicious of a plotless (or more often a badly plotted) script. It's a bit like a designer applying for a job with a portfolio of entirely abstract pieces – they may be very good, the designer may be very good, but what proof have we of any basic technical expertise? Can he or she actually draw a realistic scene in full perspective? I am always tempted to ask the writer of an abstract plotless script – well, yes, but could you just take one simple character, bring it into conflict with a specific situation and describe the result through dialogue? The truth is that this little trick lies at the heart of an ability to write successfully.

Character

To a greater or lesser extent most scripts involve the development of at least one or two central characters. A common criticism of a script is to say that the characters don't develop; that is, don't react to the movement of the plot, don't grow through experience, don't slowly reveal facets of themselves to the reader. I find it hard to imagine a successful script where our initial perception of the central characters remains entirely unaltered at the end.

The creation of character and the laughs to be gained from it are of central importance to all comedy writing and this is particularly true of television sit-com. The writer of a television series has one immediate advantage over other colleagues in the theatre or cinema and that is the building of audience familiarity. A playwright rarely has more than two or two and a half hours to set up the plot, introduce the characters, engage all the disparate elements and move the whole to a conclusion. For a screenwriter the time is normally even less. It is of course possible to create major comic characters in such a framework, characters who have become part of the common cultural heritage – one thinks immediately of Inspector Clouseau or Monsieur Hulot – but even then, both of these characters were the subject of a series of films. However, in a television series the writer has the chance to bring characters right into the home on a regular basis, sometimes over a number of years. The audience gets to know these characters as well as they know their close friends. This is of course the identical process which works to such good effect for the soaps. Interestingly enough, the comedy which has been far and away the biggest hit of recent years, *Bread*, has always seemed to me to be precisely that – a soap with the addition of a few laughs. (I hate even to suggest it, but it really is a *few* laughs we are talking about here; *Bread* is not the most gag-packed script presently on offer.)

This trick of audience recognition has allowed television sit-com to develop a style of laughter-making all of its own. After a few episodes of a well-written example the creators start to enjoy the huge dividend of the character laugh. Once the audience know that Captain Mainwaring is a pompous, self-important little turkey cock, any small incident which compromises his dignity or threatens his authority is a rich seam of laughter, which does not need funny lines as such. A look at almost any episode of *Dad's Army* will reveal huge audience enjoyment at a simple raised eyebrow from Mainwaring as Corporal Jones threatens to run amuck, or Private Pike is more than usually stupid; this is often followed by another big laugh as we cut to a close-up of Sergeant Wilson's face delicately twisted into a sneer of polite disdain.

Of course the constant inclusion of good funny dialogue can only enhance the over-all laugh ratio. The Americans are particularly good at spicing their character comedy with one-liners without straining credibility; they do this by making their character's speech patterns witty or pithy in the first place – so a Bilko or a Roseanne are exponents of quick-fire patter or the sarcastic put-down as an essential ingredient of their character make-up.

We all love to see people's real human foibles exposed and ridiculed (remember, comedy is rooted in truth) and on a personal level we rejoice when our own bank manager is discomfited. Television sit-com can convince us that we know Captain Mainwaring as well as any of our own friends and associates and so his deflation is particularly sweet. The same force is at work as Hancock's bombastic cover is blown, or Gladys Pugh's mask of respectable gentility slips, or Sergeant Bilko has to dig himself out of yet another tight corner. In television sit-com the character laugh, once it has been set up, is an enduring banker.

Situation

This leads us to the other central element of a situation comedy script – the situation itself. Nearly everyone you meet will, on being told that you are a comedy producer, suggest a good set-up for a television sitcom. A motorbike messengers' office, a novelty telegram office and a health club have been particularly popular recently. Unfortunately, this basic suggestion does not get us very far. Of course there are possibilities for comic situations in all three of these ideas – the vital messages which get confused; people in ludicrous costumes caught in strange predicaments; or fun and games in the jacuzzi (itself one of those intrinsically funny words so beloved of gag writers). They all also have that vital ingredient which shows like *Taxi* and *Cheers* exploit most successfully; they allow new characters and plot-lines to come and go virtually at random. None the less, all this potential will quickly wither on the vine unless there is a Louis or a Sam at the centre of the script.

The situation of *Dad's Army* is intrinsically funny – a group of old duffers shouldering potentially serious responsibility – but it is the way that the various characters react to this condition which generates the comedy. (To go one stage further, it is often asked what is so funny about Resistance fighters in war-torn France; well, nothing particularly, it is the characterisation of *'Allo, 'Allo* which renders the situation potentially comic.)

Sub-plots and parallel plots

Around these central requirements of plot, character and situation the writer will also need to weave other patterns. There may be sub-plots or parallel plots, both devices are common in farce; there are often diversionary scenes which interrupt the emotional flow of the main plot. There may be sudden reversals of expectation, purposely misleading developments subsequently confounded, seemingly disparate threads pulled together and sometimes just as quickly unravelled again. Over all this confusion of requirements the writer must constantly exert control.

The timing of the details of the plot development will be crucial to holding the interest of the audience; the timing of the revelation of the twists and turns of a complex central character will be essential to engaging their emotions. The rhythm of the parallel plot in relation to the main thrust of the script will ensure either that it grips the audience totally (think of Michael Palin's attempts to kill the vital old lady witness in *A Fish Called Wanda*) or that it merely confuses them. The placing of sub-scenes within the over-all framework will dictate whether it does give pause from the headlong rush of high emotion (as in the classic example of the Porter's scene in *Macbeth*) or merely irritates and distracts the reader.

Rhythm and timing

From all this two key words for the writer, any writer, become clear: rhythm and timing. Which brings us simultaneously to an old joke and to the heart of the matter. 'What is the secret of good comedy? . . . T-T-T-Timing.' The point is that timing is the secret, not only of good comedy, but of all good dramatic writing. The particular challenge facing comedy writers is that in addition to all the demands for rhythm, for timing, which they face in common with their dramatic colleagues, they have the further problem of timing the laughter.

Any comic working the tough American club circuit will quote you one golden rule: have a big laugh in your first ten seconds; they will sometimes add, then have another one every ten seconds after that. The 'hit them hard and early' theory is a good one but even in the relentless pressure cooker of the American stand-up comedy clubs, a gag of the same size and same rhythm every ten seconds would soon become wearing. The trick is to place your laughs. One of the joys of our profession is to watch a real master of the art reel in an audience; the timing of individual jokes and then their placement within the over-all rhythm of the entire act lies at the heart of the technique of a Jack Benny or a Tommy Cooper. Watch Dave Allen tickle out a long anecdotal story with smaller laughs, throw-away observations, little strokes of in-fill colouring, until by the time he gets to the big punchline the audience are so tantalised by the wait that the final explosive roar is guaranteed.

The same technique applies to a comedy script. Anticipating the eventual laugh pattern is crucial. I have often suggested a simple exercise to a new writer whose script I have read; take a magic marker and go through the script page by page marking where you think the laughs will be. Use, say, red for the big belly laughs and blue for the ticklers. If you are really harsh with yourself and refuse to mark puns (which although they can add colour and detail to the text rarely get a good audience response), 'funny' names of people or places and old music hall gags reworked into the dialogue, you will, sometimes disarmingly, reveal the true state of your script. More often than not with unsolicited comedy material this exercise will leave several pages untouched by the marker pen. (It is not uncommon for a whole script to reveal not a single real laugh.) If you calculate that a page of dialogue will play for thirty to forty-five seconds then clearly a single page with no mark on it had better have other good reasons for being there – we all know it takes a lot of dialogue to set up new characters and new situations, the trick is making the stuff funny at the same time.

Presuming we now have a script with a good solid collection of laughs, the next question is what size of laugh and where do they come in the script? Remembering the old American comic's adage, a couple of solid reds on page one are always welcome even if not absolutely essential. By the same token pages one–six thinly splattered with blue has to be a danger sign.

A final requirement is to balance the size and frequency of the laughter. Of course all this is somewhat speculative at the early stages but it is normally possible to distinguish (even on the cold page) between the huge crescendo of laughter which should greet Basil Fawlty's assault on his stalled motor car and the smaller giggles afforded by his rude asides to Sybil. The huge guffaw has to be built for and allowed to subside and the gentler laugh used to colour in the spaces, in just the same way as the rhythm and impetus of a piece of music ebb and flow. The *1812 Overture* wouldn't work if the fireworks and cannon went off in the first bar and continued throughout.

I've taken some space trying to explain the rhythm of laughter in a comedy script, not because it's the most important of all the rhythms at work but because it is the special extra discipline for which the comedy writer has to allow. In the most successful comedy writing the speed at which the plot and the characters reveal themselves are perfectly balanced by the rhythm of the waves of laughter, so that emphasis is given to both the dramatic information and the comedy, just as the rhythm of a successful poem emphasises its emotion or its sense.

I have been dissecting the workings of a comedy script in a way which is certain to provoke an accusation of rather dry, theoretical dogmatism. So many writers and performers when asked why they are funny will say with real feeling, I don't know and I don't want to analyse it, I just do what comes naturally and don't think about it too much. It is certainly true that the kind of examination I have been conducting is a retrospective exercise, a look at why a finished piece of writing either works or doesn't. At the end of the day I suspect that one sits down and gets the text on to paper before going back to check the flow of events. The rhythm will have come naturally and if it hasn't, mathematical calculations of when the next gag is due or the next plot device is needed are unlikely to help.

In any event, perhaps I should close on a more practical note. Of course the presentation of work is important – a neatly typed, well-spaced script is quite simply easier to read than a handwritten scrawl. However, if a script gets read and it is funny I doubt whether worries about the quality of the paper will damage its chances. I have just signed my contract for this chapter and attached to it are four pages of notes from the BBC about typeface, spelling conventions, punctuation, etc. It includes the warning 'We will reject single-line spaced copy.' Well, from me probably yes, but I seem to remember that from Dylan Thomas the BBC were only too pleased to accept *Under Milk Wood* scrawled on the back of beer mats which the producer collected from various taverns around London's West End.

I certainly prefer to read easy, clean copy and there comes a point beyond which scrawl is indecipherable but at the end of the day the truth of this business is summed up in the old Hollywood adage: you need just three things to make a good film; first a good script, second a good script and third a good script. If the laughs aren't coming no level of neatness can compensate but if you can make them roll in the aisles with guaranteed accuracy time and again, you will soon be able to pay a whole typing pool to get your words of wisdom down on paper.

Adaptations

Jeanette Winterson

A woman goes into an art gallery. She sees a vase and falls in love with it. She goes over to the sculptor and tells her how much she loves her work; the colour, the shape, the glaze, the particular wholeness of the piece. Naturally the sculptor is flattered. 'Yes,' says the woman, getting out her cheque book, 'your work is unique. Now, could you just smash it up and make me six cups and saucers out of it?'

When it was suggested that I might like to make my first novel, *Oranges are Not the Only Fruit*, into a three-part drama for BBC Television, I was delighted. A year later, the scripts completed and the project ready to be filmed, I am still delighted, but there have been many peaks and troughs along the way. It is those peaks and troughs that I wish to record. In the true style of *Pilgrim's Progress*, a journey very similar to my own, I will begin with a word of warning. Every writer needs a head for heights, but only those who can also stomach the abyss had better think of working for film and television.

The first question for anyone transposing a book to the screen, is how to smash up the original and do it justice in a different way. Faithful adaptations make bad television. It's better to have a new vision that is faithful to the spirit of the work, without worrying about fitting everything in, or even keeping the same order of events.

Time and place can be altered, if those elements are not crucial to the truth of the tale. For instance, it does no harm to play Shakespeare as you like it, but it would by unhelpful to take a novel about a mining community in Wales and set it in the Green Belt. A scriptwriter must be honest about any changes he or she makes. Do they work towards a perfect whole, or are the changes just a bit of tinkering? As the writer of both the novel and the scripts, I was not in the business of tinkering, but I knew that real changes had to be made to my experimental, in many ways anti-linear, novel to render it the kind of television that would bring viewers in off the streets. At the same time, I did not want to destroy at a stroke all the nuances, subtleties, games and cumulative effects that are the pleasures of well-written prose. I didn't want to lose anything and I wanted to gain a lot. What was to be done? My immediate task was to identify the difference between real losses and fond farewells. The fairy tales and allegorical passages that weave themselves within the main story could be waved goodbye without any pain because their function could be taken over by the camera itself. They worked as a kind of Greek Chorus commenting on the main events. The camera, with its silent ability to offer other dimensions to what appears to be happening, works as a mute Greek Chorus. The power of the image means that you don't always have to spell it out.

It was also necessary to decide what parts of the book were irrelevant to the story I had decided to tell on television. This is a question which dogs all scrupulous scriptwriters because a novel is often full of attendant passages which are not the story as such, but which are in themselves pleasurable. Inevitably some of these will have to go, if only so that the main theme can enjoy full development. Having done the hatchet work, the scriptwriter must try and heal the wounds by conveying along with the camera a sense of the scope of the original piece. In *Oranges*, I did my best to offer a consistently surreal world view to make up for the flights of fancy and the suggestiveness of language that I had felt could not be included. One of my favourite passages in the novel, a short essay on the differences between history and story-telling, entitled 'Deuteronomy', had to be left out. And yet it is central to the book and no accident that it falls precisely in the middle of the seven chapters. What I hope I have managed to do, is dissolve it and scatter it throughout the three episodes. The characters are always telling stories, to each other, about themselves, even to themselves, and set against this is the notion of history, objectivity, fact. In virtually every scene there are at least two definitions of reality at work. No single line is directed, though sympathies are suggested. What the viewer must do is to pick her way through this multiplicity of truth and time and decide what to believe. I think this properly conveys the simple though highly complex statement which is true of the book obliquely and that chapter very clearly;

namely, I am lying to you but I am also telling you the truth. Trust me.

I didn't find it easy to break down my novel into three fifty-minute episodes, each complete in itself but leading temptingly to the next one. Naturally the ending of each had to be very strong. It's not alien to write a novel in this way, Dickens did it all the time, but if it's not your style, the transition presents problems. Very few books divide themselves neatly into same-length episodes and so a scriptwriter must be very careful to get the balance and pacing right. In many places I had to alter the sequence of events, stretch out some scenes, compress others and always be aware of the over-all emphasis I wanted. It's an obvious trap to fall into, when writing in parts, to concentrate on them as individual exercises and forget about the shape of the whole. Nevertheless, it is the whole on which we will be judged.

There is something fantastically artificial about trying to chop up a work with supermarket efficiency into nice same-sized chunks. It's not usually written or read that way. If it had been possible I would have preferred the episodes to have been different lengths; as it was I decided to accept the restrictions as a challenge and to see whether or not an internal time-rhythm could be set up that flouted the one I had been given.

Episode one is in respect of two and three quite leisurely. The characters are introduced without haste, without cramming, and we become accustomed to them and their habits without a great deal of 'action'. I don't overload the viewer with plot because I'm asking him or her to get to know my people. Once that's happened, I can fall into a kind of shorthand, the way we do with our friends, so that much can be transmitted by a little. My characters are not figures who act out a plot; they are the plot. Therefore it seemed right to weigh out the episodes differently, so that in the beginning we have enough room to know whom we're dealing with. This left the remaining episodes with a lot of ground to cover; the internal rhythm speeds up and intensifies until the very end of episode three, when a sudden slowing down creates a poignancy that is not only what the camera is doing or what the words are doing, but what the structure itself has made possible.

It is vital, then, when considering how to divide up the material you have chosen to include, to give serious attention to the internal time-rhythm and how it can contribute to the effect you are aiming for. It is a much more subliminal device than the others we are thinking about but just as powerful. Thirty minutes or fifty minutes a week is what you've got, but how you use it, how you stretch it or shrink it, is up to you. I believe, too, that concentration on the internal time-rhythm gets round the problem of sacrificing the depth of a novel to its pace. In my blackest hours, before I really hit on how to weight the thing, I felt like a hack porn writer who must put in a bit of sex every ten pages. Of course the thing has to be kept moving and above all we don't want our audience going off to make a cup of tea because they think nothing's going on, but movement doesn't mean action every moment. Let's not forget that art is about space.

What about language? So often the neglected sister of the big brother, the image. Words are my passion and I didn't want the dialogue of *Oranges* to sound like so much television-speak (and film-speak, to be fair). By that, I mean the dreary naturalism that is usually interpreted as realism. Naturalism and realism need not be the same thing. Harold Pinter and Alan Bennett both use highly artificial dialogue, sentences and shapes of sentences that one never encounters in real life, and yet their work is realistic in that it reflects common situations and reveals human emotions. Too many writers, in all media, struggle for realism and all they get is naturalism; flat, unapproachable situations, language so long dead it doesn't even smell anymore. For the screenwriter, this is a serious problem, especially since we have more than a sneaking suspicion that the audience only wants the pictures anyway.

But we cut our own throats. If we don't give them anything worth listening to, why should they listen? Most television drama and indeed most films could still be accompanied by the piano only, and no one would be any worse off. We have to find a language that is vibrant. A language that is the equal partner of the image. When adapting a work that does not depend on dialogue for its effects, the temptation is to overwrite; to shove into the mouth of any vaguely suitable character the impressions and persuasions that have been achieved in the novel by other means. It is usually better to let the camera stand in for those other means and to keep the dialogue free from weights it cannot bear. I do not mean by this that dialogue is a frivolous device unable to handle important material, but the flow of conversation must be precisely that: a flow, not a jam of information fighting for air.

We live in a society where more has become interchangeable with better, and we see this as much in writing as we do in the individual's determination to have everything, even if she doesn't want it. More words don't of themselves mean more power. A few words, perfectly timed and in the right place, can have exactly the effect the writer wants, tears, laughter, a sudden shift of sympathy. I'm not advocating great tracts of silence, simply urging us to consider what the words are doing and whether we're using them well. In television or film, sloppy language is as unacceptable as sloppy camerawork, though the latter seems to worry people more.

My own solution to the problem of over-writing, a problem which persisted in some areas, even after I had identified what the camera could do without any help from me, was to keep the exchanges between characters unnaturally short. No one watching casually will notice this technique, namely my remarks about naturalism and realism, but it works very well and makes certain that nothing is made too obvious or too tedious. Even in long scenes the movement from one character to the other or others is rapid. I don't leave room for any of them to use words they don't need. They are to the point without seeming spartan. Whenever I wrote a scene, I went back over it and took away redundancy and excess. I do this continually in my novel-writing and it seemed proper to take such pains with dialogue, where the relative monotony of having only one major literary device at my disposal sometimes made me careless. Short exchanges have a further bonus; should you choose to depart from that technique for a while, the effect of a soliloquy or a few longueurs is greatly heightened. The change of rhythm adds to the power of the moment you wish to stand out.

Radio drama, very satisfactory in its own right, is excellent training for scriptwriters. Adaptations are usually first-rate and much can be learned from reading the work in question, then carefully investigating why the adaptation is a success. What techniques are being used and could they transfer to the screen? On the radio, there are no pictures, except for the ones the words can create in the listener's imagination. This makes it an exacting medium and one where any verbal insecurity is immediately obvious. It is interesting to note that the presence of a narrator in most adaptations is designed to free the dialogue from unnecessary drag in much the same way as the camera does on screen.

What can we expect from language? Everything. Just as there are no bad dogs, only bad trainers, so there is no bad language, only bad writers. Why devise language at all? To communicate. To communicate what? Shopping list needs and directions and advice about the weather are soon soaked up by a very few words and the rudiments of grammar. So what are we to do with the richness that remains? Ignore it? Neglect it? Or ride it like a racehorse through every kind of country? The more we ask of language, the more we shall receive. I think it is incumbent upon any scriptwriter to use language well; to recognise that if the script itself is powerful, without any of the benefits of actors and director and all the alchemy that takes place on set, the finished product is likely to be outstanding. This matters. We do not need any more mediocre television.

Please do not misunderstand me; all of the arts are suffering from a bad bout of mediocrity. Television, uncertain of its own credentials and forced to fill up a blank screen every moment of the day and night, is bound to suffer more than the less-pressed custodians of culture. If television is here to stay, and it seems to be, we must demand of it the very best possible as often as possible. That means demanding of ourselves, as scriptwriters, the very best. The script should be the foundation of the finished product, not the rough guide or endlessly reworked blueprint, sometimes so endlessly reworked that it bears no resemblance to what the writer had in mind. A 'so-so' script just begs to be treated in an off-hand manner; if it's full of holes, then the only person who'll fall through them is the writer. Meanwhile, the director and the cast will sew it up between them.

Ideally, of course, there will be complete collaboration between workers on the team and that has certainly been my experience. However, I've talked to other writers whose experience has not been anything like as harmonious and whose presence has been viewed as 'a necessary evil'. I do believe that a strong script makes that impossible. Our job is to make the most triumphant thing we can and then step back to allow the director and cast and all the great machine to bring their vision to it. We can't expect them to cover up for our inadequacies.

There have been times during the scripting of *Oranges* when I have been tempted to take short cuts. When I have not always been ready to search for the right word in the right place and when I have made the excuse that dialogue passes so swiftly that no one will notice all of it anyway. The longer the project, the more likely this is to be a problem. We all remember one-liners but the rest, the bulk of what we hear, seems to pass unnoticed, as eclipsed by the images as ghosts in daylight. A salutary experience for me was attending the read-through of my three episodes. Even if the whole world was determined not to hear a thing, what was certain was that the actors remember every word. And it matters to them. Language matters to them. Dustin Hoffman didn't come over to play Shylock for pocket money just because he felt like being on the stage. By his own admission he wanted lines that were worth learning.

I shall come down from my orange box. At the end of his journey, Pilgrim, having passed through The Valley of Temptation, The Slough of Despond and many other pitfalls, comes into the wide and generous light of the company of angels and realises that throughout his trials he was never really alone. The others were standing by. I suppose that's what I discovered above all; how collaborative it can be and how worthwhile it is when that works. It makes sense of all those lonely hours at the typewriter, all the pages thrown away because they're good but not good enough. If in doubt, remember, the company are not far off.

Foot in the Door – Minimum Bruising

Roger Gregory

Access to television? Where to send your script? Simple: note the name of the writer or script editor, or the producer or director, and write to him or her care of the television company that made the programme you have just watched.

Of course, it is not that simple. The energy, commitment and willpower involved in writing the script must be matched with equal quantities of application and ingenuity as you set about gaining attention for your writing. Of the script editor, writer, director and producer, only the script editor is likely to be still working at the same company by the time the programme is transmitted many months after production.

The producer is the only member of the team likely to be able to progress your work towards production. The producer will be hedged about with script readers, consultants and script departments busily reading your script and deciding whether to bring it to the producer's attention. Often the producer was once a script editor and will now have a network of writer contacts to turn to for material.

The director tends to be placed outside the development process unless particular working relationships dictate otherwise.

Script editors can recommend and enthuse over a particular script but cannot ultimately ensure its production.

Writers have their own fish to fry, and a living to make. You will learn more from them when they lecture on a writing course (see 'Learn the business', p. 68), when you will have the opportunity to discuss your work with them.

Study the form

Breaking into the television market is not simply a matter of knowing where to send a script and the correct address of the relevant company. You cannot sit at home writing in quiet moments and send the results off and assume your job is done. It is only just beginning. A serious contender for a writing career in television will be an avid watcher of television and films, and a theatre-goer. You should make notes, keep lists and collate the information collected.

Programme information sources

To find out who was responsible for past programmes from the BBC, you can contact the BBC Radio Programme Information Unit on 01-580 4468 ext. 3048, or Television Information Office on 01-743 8000 ext. 5075. The IBA has an Information Service about ITV and Channel 4 programmes (01-534 7011). The BFI number is 01-255 1444 for details of cinema and television going back to about 1976. The ICA offers a public access video library and provides cheap viewing opportunities (01-930 3647).

Periodicals and Directories

You need to develop a knowledge of the market place and to this end you must get to know the people in the business even if only through the gossip, articles, production announcements and career moves in the trade papers. Fortunately, most of these can be seen at your local library since subscribing to even the short list here would be expensive.

Besides the obvious necessity of the *Radio Times* and *TV Times*, *The Listener* provides a weekly back section of comment, reviews and previews. Over the last few years it has involved itself very much with the debate over cable and satellite television and the government's attempts at new legislation. *Broadcast* and *Television Week* can be read more quickly and contain news and production information, notes on who is working where and information about over-all company moves and plans. Any properly informed writer for television would also have an eye on the world of film as well as that of theatre. Thus the BFI's *Sight and Sound* for discussion and opinion and *Screen International* for basic regular information are worth looking at. There are many other film magazines attempting a variety of approaches to film. The BFI also has a library service for members.

The grandmother of them all, *Stage and Television Today*, provides a weekly pot-pourri of gossip, reviews and useful information if read assiduously, but selectively. Those with the time might like to add *Variety* to their weekly reading list.

One annual publication well worth buying and referring to before despatching your script is *Contacts*. Published by *Spotlight* (01-437 7631), it covers 'stage, television, screen and radio' and lists contacts for literary agents, actors' agents, theatre companies and directors, and the senior personnel of all the television companies in as much detail as the individual companies choose to supply. These details will enable you to personalise your submission and help you begin to put together a map of how the people in the world of drama interconnect.

Learn the business

There are a great many courses for would-be writers. You must first disentangle the schools of journalism from the array on offer. Creative writing courses range from university options to evening classes. Courses run by professional practitioners – writers, script editors, producers – are the ones to look for if you are in the business of submitting work for television production. Even better if, due to your study of the form, you recognise the names of the tutors and know something of their writing and the themes they tackle.

The Arvon Foundation (040-923 338), Totleigh Barton, Sheepwash, Beaworthy, Devon EX21 5NS, provides five-day residential groups for up to sixteen people. These courses cover a whole range of writing disciplines but do have some related to television drama and radio drama which are run by duos of writers or a writer/producer or script editor team.

Film Schools and Media Study Courses These are graduate and postgraduate courses for which grants are often available. Creative writing is likely to be only a part of any of these courses if it figures at all. It is noticeable at many graduate film showings how vulnerable the film-maker is without access to accomplished writing.

The London Screenwriters Workshop (01-883 7218), 64 Church Crescent, London N10 3NE, was set up by a group of aspiring film and television writers in 1983. They quickly moved from reading and criticising one another's scripts to improving their knowledge of, and contact with, the industry by inviting speakers from the world of film and television. The Workshop is not a training organisation *per se*, rather it is a support group which helps screenwriters gain access to the industry. It does run a programme of seminars and workshops throughout the year and issues a regular newsletter to members. An offshoot of the main activities are the intensive workshops where a group of writers are supervised by an experienced screenwriter as they develop an idea into a completed script under the tough scrutiny of the other writers. Once it is deemed marketable, advice is given on how best to achieve it.

Robert McKee, who was a story editor at UA and NBC and who has written numerous scripts, visits Britain with an intensive three-day seminar for writers on story structure. His last visit was heavily oversubscribed. For information on his next visit ring Joan Harrison of International Forum (0732 810561).

The BBC Script Unit (01-743 8000), 252 Western Avenue, Acton, London W3 6XJ, initiates various projects for developing writing talent. These are by invitation and are based on unsolicited material submitted in the normal way to the Script Unit. The readers for the Unit are encouraged to meet writers whose work they feel shows promise. Although the Unit does not commission and does not work to drama producers, it can go some way towards guiding new writers and provide useful forums for discussion and training.

Examples of the projects initiated recently by the Script Unit are: a search for five- or ten-minute scripts for use on the BBC Directors Training Course, a link with a London Drama School to produce staged versions of plays written for the television studio, and play readings to workshop selected plays with the writers and actors.

Apart from specific schemes like the one run by the BBC Script Unit, and a one-off campaign like *Debut on Two*, there is no real market for the short script and uncommissioned writers would do better to concentrate on work for the conventional sixty-minute and ninety-minute slots.

Mohammed and mountains

There is every argument for pursuing producers and production companies that seem to choose material and themes similar to your own. However, you risk rejection on the grounds of similarity if you slavishly follow the style and content of the output from your target company.

Most companies have anonymous systems for receiving and processing unsolicited scripts. Note 'processing': scripts are not necessarily read all through. Many production companies limit their reading to scripts submitted via agents or from other sources where it can be assumed some judgment has been exercised over the script before it reaches them. So if you cannot get to them, what better than to have them come to you? There are other ways to get their attention besides trying to penetrate the screen around them with a script through the post. Every production unit, however populist and busy, is aware of the need to generate and test new writers. They will keep their eye on all likely sources of writing talent: theatre, journalism, novels, film school productions and radio drama.

One of the most rewarding sources of new writing potential is the *Fringe Theatre*. The fact of a production here guarantees the material produced has come through some kind of slection process and has had some of its dramatic potential tested in rehearsal.

Scouts for television, film and radio will keep a close watch on what happens in the fringe theatre and what they see may well persuade them to contact you. Having your work taken up by a fringe company may seem as remote as the chances of being commissioned by a television company. However, theatrical mythology of the seventies is littered with stories of people who set up their own companies with limited funds, often with the aim of providing an outlet for their own writing.

There are also highly professional *amateur theatre companies* in many parts of the country offering the chance to practise the craft of dramatist as well as providing the opportunity to explore the full range of theatre disciplines. For details of your nearest company contact the National Operatic and Dramatic Association (01-837 5655), 1 Crestfield Street, London WC1H 8AV.

The largest annual output of drama must be that produced by the BBC for its *Radio Drama* Department. The annual output is over 300 plays of various lengths plus classic serialisations and modern original serials. Thus the demand for material is much greater than any other medium and producers are constantly looking to add to the list of new accomplished writers. Radio Drama editors, and producers too, attend to every possible source of new material. Much radio drama production is based in the regions. A new writer has the chance to make personal contact with the drama producers based locally. The producers in their turn will be looking for plays which reflect in some way the region they originate from and engage with non-metropolitan issues, to propose to the editors based in London at Broadcasting House. Of course, radio plays are no easier to write than any other kind of drama, nor is a facility with radio drama necessarily any guarantee that a writer can think and write in the visual and filmic way demanded for television writing. But as a means of gaining experience of the production process – rehearsals, actors' reactions to your dialogue, director's analysis – radio drama is unsurpassed and people involved in drama listen with a professional ear cocked.

Journalism and novels probably yield stories and ideas rather than potential new writers. The novelist has recourse to so many levels of narrative exposition and character delineation that are denied the dramatist, who must trust his audience to understand or at least relish the enigmatic revelations that come from dialogue unsupported by a narrative voice.

Know yourself

If you develop the necessary critical instincts to be able to aim your work at the most receptive market, you must also focus that critical eye on your own work as though it were written by someone else.

This process should move rapidly from an analysis of the type of material you write, the style and the recurring themes, to a detailed examination of tone, rhythms, effects attempted and achieved, characterisation through dialogue, and clarity. But do not bore the reader with all this analysis. They are not interested in the mechanics of your script.

What the script should do is enable the reader to visualise the film that will eventually be made. So description must be vivid but not wordy, the juxtaposition of images clear without resort to writing a shooting script. A 'movie in the head' for the reader.

Research as an antidote to writer's block

Research means work. You cannot draw on your imagination or personal experiences and then just write. You have to get facts, check details, find local colour and sift cultural differences. When you do enough research, the story will almost write itself. Writer's block occurs when the writer has nothing to say and cannot bring the characters to life because they are still unknown, unexplored. The best cure for writer's block is research. Stop creating and go exploring.

Chameleon scripts

Don't ever send your script saying you know there is more work to be done, nor, even worse, offer to make it longer or shorter, a single or a series, on demand. When you send it it must be clear both to you and the people who will read it why every line is as it is and why every scene is essential to your planned development of the structure. Of course, other voices will eventually influence further rewrites of the script. These will come from script editors, producers, directors and actors. Sometimes they will be more interested in forming your script into something they have in their own head, but there will be occasions when artistic and practical considerations will argue for changes. All of this is part of the natural process through which a script progresses to production.

Buck the system – but play by the rules

Most standard works on writing for television, where they attempt advice on submitting scripts, tend to reflect the research the author of the book has undertaken. Thus the process suggested for submitting a script is likely to be the typical process used by the majority of the television companies to deal with unsolicited material. Your job as an aspiring writer is to avoid having your script 'processed' and prevent it from being treated like the hundreds of others.

A script unit of experienced readers 'weeding' unsolicited scripts is unlikely to miss potential. But they are not in the business of getting programmes made. They deal with thousands of unsolicited scripts which come in every year. All they do is read your script and if in their opinion it warrants a second read pass it to other readers and script editors. By all means use their services to gain feedback but do not expect too much detail in their response. For ways in which the BBC Script Unit offers more than this basic service, see 'Learn the business', p. 68.

If you are to gain full advantage from your study of form, you should hope to please the individual taste of a particular producer. It is certainly worth ringing the company to check the name of the producer's script editor, asking about production plans and telling them to expect your script. Do not ask what they are looking for. The answer will always be: 'the best and most suitable script available'.

Some practicalities

Layout

Scripts must be typed. Even the best handwriting – laborious to produce – is still noticeably more difficult to read, and when you are reading up to ten scripts a day, this matters. Beyond the typing, they must be clearly laid out. Do not make maximum use of the page in the interest of economy. Only type on one side of the paper.

At this early submission stage it is not necessary to follow slavishly the examples of layout provided in some books on the subject. It must be clear who is speaking, and what we are seeing at any given moment. This in itself can be a complicated process. The acquisition of some shorthand initials (OOV – Out of vision; VO – Voice over; etc.) can save time and typewriter ribbon. These and their functions can be gleaned while reading the many published television plays and the increasing number of feature film scripts available. Clarity of expression and the entertaining (in the broadest sense of the word) nature of your script when read is all part of the test you are undergoing. It is not that you must tell us how to react and what to feel, but it must be clear what you think of the characters and situations in your play.

Copyright and confidentiality

Mark your script © and put the date on it along with your name and contact address. Then, in the unlikely event that your authorship is challenged, you can prove the date of copyright from the copy you will have lodged with a bank or solicitor. The ACTT and Writers' Guild provide a script registration service for members. All this may seem an elaborate, even costly, process. You must decide how important the protection of your copyright is to you at this early stage in your writing career.

You can also keep some control over the circumstances in which you tell producers your ideas. You need to establish the confidentiality of the conversation. Since the *Rock Follies* judgement this confidential telling of ideas does protect the owner of the original idea. Of course there are occasions when similar ideas clash on a producer's desk. If, when you are one-fifth into the telling, the producer tells you there is something similar on offer already then you can reasonably trust that this is coincidence. It is much easier to prove breach of confidence than breach of copyright. Therefore, if you genuinely feel anxious, it is better that you put in any covering letter and on top o the script the words: 'in confidence'.

Agents

Literary agents are listed, if they so choose, in *Contacts* and in the *Writers' and Artists' Yearbook*. You will have to be at quite an advanced stage of your study of the form before you will be able to discuss the relative strengths and specialist interests of the agents listed. Agents like television companies use readers to help them deal with unsolicited material. Their low profile relative to the television companies means that scripts that reach them have already gone through some form of filter. This being the case the agent is likely to spend some time reading unsolicited material and will not automatically pass it on to a reader. If they like your work they will suggest rewrites or give you advice about where to send it. They would have to like it a lot to offer to send it out on your behalf. A telephone call to check if they are an agency which is interested in encouraging new talent may save postage and unnecessary rejection.

When sending scripts to an agent you should always enclose a synopsis and a stamped addressed envelope. If you haven't heard from them after six weeks a polite phone call should be made. After another six weeks, the enquiry should be a little less polite.

Writers' organisations

Writers' Guild of Great Britain (01-723 8074) is the writers' trade union, affiliated to the TUC and representing writers' interests in film, radio, theatre, television and publishing. The Guild gives help and advice to members on all aspects of their business life including contracts, agents, television companies and fees. Theirs are the agreements that regulate the minimum fees for television drama within the BBC and the commercial companies. They have also recently negotiated agreements with the British Film and Television Producers Association and The Independent Programme Producers Association to cover film and independent television screen writing. The Guild issues a Directory of Members.

The Society of Authors (01-373 6642) has a permanent staff including a solicitor and can give a comprehensive personal and professional service covering the business aspects of authorship. Besides providing information on agents and publishers they will advise writers without an agent on a contract. They will also take up complaints on behalf of their members. They hold weekend conferences and seminars and publish a range of extremely practical books and guides for writers which are free to members. Their bias is towards help for novelists whereas the Writers' Guild seems to do more work regarding script writers.

Theatre Writers' Union (Al Hunter on 01-582 3927), as its title suggests, is for theatre writers, and is active in providing courses and advice on a regional basis. The regional groups can be reached via the London telephone number.

ACTT Writers' Section (01-437 8506): current Chairman of the Writers' Section is Alistair Beaton.

The New Playwrights Trust (London) (01-377 5429), based at Whitechapel library, provides excellent information in the form of a monthly newsletter, a script/writer registration service, a script reading service and a bulletin which is distributed to all London's major pub theatres as well as other companies, theatres and agents. This is a regional as well as a London network.

North West Playwrights (061-274 3434), based at the Contact Theatre, Manchester, offer similar services and have been running a workshop for new writers for the past seven years.

New Playwriting Scotland (c/o Ella Wildridge, 22 Castle Square, Kingskettle, Fife KY7 7PP) provides an information broadsheet and a Playwrights' Register for Scotland.

Bibliography

Published television plays

Many of these texts will only be available through libraries.

JOHN ARDEN, *Soldier, Soldier*; *Wet Fish* in *Soldier, Soldier*, Methuen, 1967.

HOWARD BARKER, *Heroes of Labour* in *Gambit Magazine*, 29, Calder and Boyars, 1976.
Pity in History in *Gambit Magazine*, 41, John Calder, 1984.

ALAN BENNETT, *Talking Heads* (monologues for television), BBC Books, 1988.
An Englishman Abroad, in *Objects of Affection and other plays for television*, BBC Publications, 1982.
The Writer in Disguise (plays), Faber and Faber, 1985.

MAEVE BINCHY, *Deeply Regretted*, Dublin Toroe Press, 1979.

ANDREW BIRKIN, *The Lost Boys*, BBC Publications, 1980.

ALAN BLEASDALE, *The Boys from the Blackstuff* (scripts), Granada, 1983.
Videos, BFI Film and VT Library.
The Monocled Mutineer, Hutchinson, 1986.

JOHN BOWEN, *The Essay Prize*; *A Holiday Abroad*; *The Candidate* in *The Essay Prize*, Faber and Faber, 1968.
Robin Redbreast in *The Television Dramatist*, Elek, 1973.
Heil Caesar, BBC Publications, 1974.

MALCOLM BRADBURY (WITH CHRISTOPHER BIGSBY), *The After Dinner Game* (four plays for television). Also includes *Love on a Gunpoint*, *Standing in for Henry* and *The Enigma*. Arrow Books, 1989.

HOWARD BRENTON, *The Saliva Milkshake* (stage version), TQ
  Publications, 1977.
  Dead Head, Methuen, 1987.

PADDY CHAYEFSKY, *Printer's Measure* in *Conflicting Generations*,
  Longman, 1968.

ROY CLARKE, *The Last of the Summer Wine* (7 scripts), BBC Publications,
  1976.

DAVID CREGAN, *Miniatures* (stage version), Methuen, 1970.
  George Reborn in *The Land of Palms*, Eyre Methuen, 1973.

IAN CURTEIS, *Long Voyage Out of War*, Calder and Boyars, 1971.
  Churchill and the Generals, BBC Publications, 1980.
  Suez, BBC Publications, 1980.
  The Falklands Play, Hutchinson, 1987.

WALLY K. DALY, *Butterflies Don't Count*, Eyre Methuen, 1978.

KEITH DEWHURST, *Z Cars* (script), Longman, 1968.

ANN DEVLIN, *The Long March, A Woman Calling* in *Ourselves Alone*, Faber
  and Faber, 1988.

CLIVE EXTON, *No Fixed Abode* in *Six Granada Plays*, Faber and Faber,
  1960.

RONALD EYRE, *The Victim* in *Conflicting Generations*, Longman, 1968.
  Z Cars (script), Longman, 1968.

CHRISTOPHER FRY, *The Brontës of Haworth*, Davis-Poynter, 1975
  (2 vols.).

GALTON and SIMPSON, *Hancock's Half Hour*, Woburn Press, 1974/
  Futura, 1975.

NADINE GORDIMER, *A Chip of Ruby Glass* in *Living Together*, Heinemann,
  1986.

SIMON GRAY, *Sleeping Dog*, Faber and Faber, 1968.
  Spoiled (stage version), Methuen, 1971.
  Plaintiffs and Defendants; *Two Sundays* in *Otherwise Engaged*, Eyre
    Methuen, 1975.
  Man in a Side Car; *Molly* (stage version of *Death of a Teddy Bear*) in
    The Rear Column, Eyre Methuen, 1978.
  Pig in a Poke in *Close of Play & Pig in a Poke*, Eyre Methuen, 1975.
  After Pilkington, Methuen, 1987.

LEON GRIFFITHS, *Dinner at the Sporting Club*, Eyre Methuen, 1978.

TREVOR GRIFFITHS, *All Good Men*; *Absolute Beginners*, Faber and Faber, 1977.
Through the Night; *Such Impossibilities*, Faber and Faber, 1977.

TOM HADDAWAY, *The Filleting Machine* in *Three North East Plays*, Iron Press, 1976, and *Act Three*, Hutchinson, 1979.

CHRISTOPHER HAMPTON, *Abel's Will*, Faber and Faber, 1979.

DAVID HARE, *Licking Hitler*, Faber and Faber, 1978.
Dreams of Leaving, Faber and Faber, 1980.

RICHARD HARRIS, *Reasonable Suspicion* in *The Pressures of Life*, Longman, 1977.

JIM HAWKINS, *Too Hot to Handle* in *Three One-Act Plays*, Amber Lane Press, 1979.

BARRY HINES, *Speech Day* in *Prompt Two*, Hutchinson, 1976, and *The Pressures of Life*, Longmans, 1977.
Two Men From Derby in *Act Two*, Hutchinson, 1979.
The Price of Coal, Hutchinson, 1979.

JOHN HOPKINS, *Talking to a Stranger*, Penguin, 1967.
A Game – Like – Only a Game in *Conflicting Generations*, Longman, 1968.
Z Cars (script), Longman, 1968.

TERRY JOHNSON, *Time Trouble and Tuesday's Child* (with Kate Lock), Methuen, 1987.

JULIA JONES, *Still Waters* (plays), Longman, 1978.

NIGEL KNEALE, *The Road*; *The Year of the Sex Olympics*; *The Stone Tape* in *The Year of the Sex Olympics*, Ferret Fantasy, 1976.

CARLA LANE, *Episodes from The Liver Birds* in *Situation Comedy*, Studio, 1980.

HENRY LIVINGS, *There's No Room for You Here as a Start* in *Kelly's Eye*, Methuen, 1964.

PETER MCDOUGAL, *Loyalties* in *Act Two*, Hutchinson, 1979.

IAN MCEWAN, *Solid Geometry* in *The Imitation Game: Three Plays for Television*, Cape, 1981.
The Ploughman's Lunch, Methuen, 1985.

DAVID MERCER, *Collected Television Plays* (2 vols.), John Calder, 1981.

PAULA MILNE, *Expectations* in *Juliet Bravo*, Longman, 1983.

GRAYGNA MONVID, *Choices, 4 Plays for ITV's 'Starting Out' Series*, *Spotlights*, Heinemann, 1986.

ELAINE MORGAN, *The Soldier and The Woman*, French, 1961.

JOHN MORTIMER, *Call Me A Liar* in *Lunch Hour*, Methuen, 1977.
David and Broccoli in *Conflicting Generations*, Longman, 1968.
A Choice of Kings (stage version) in *Playbill Three*, Hutchinson Educational, 1969.

PETER NICHOLS, *Promenade* in *Six Granada Plays*, Faber and Faber, 1960.
The Gorge in *The Television Dramatist*, Elek, 1973.

JOHN OSBORNE, *A Subject of Scandal and Concern*, Faber and Faber, 1961.
The Right Prospectus, Faber and Faber, 1970.
The Gift of Friendship, Faber and Faber, 1972.
Jill and Jack in *The End of Me Old Cigar*, Faber and Faber, 1975.
You're Not Watching Me, Mummy; *Try A Little Tenderness*, Faber and Faber, 1978.

TONY PARKER, *Mrs Lawrence Will Look After It*; *Chariot of Fire*; *When The Bow Breaks* in *Three TV Plays*, Davis-Poynter, 1975.

CARYL PHILLIPS, *Playing Away*, Faber and Faber, 1986.

HAROLD PINTER, *A Night Out* in *A Slight Ache*, Methuen, 1961.
The Collection; *The Lover*, Methuen, 1963.
Tea Party; *The Basement*; *Night School* in *Tea Party*, Methuen, 1967.

ALAN PLATER, *Annie Kenney* (*Shoulder to Shoulder*) in *Act Three*, Hutchinson, 1979.
Z Cars (script), Longman, 1968.

CHERRY POTTER, *The Protectors* in *Power*, Studio, 1981.

DENNIS POTTER, *The Nigel Barton Plays*, Penguin, 1967.
Son of Man (stage version), Penguin, 1971.
Follow the Yellow Brick Road in *The Television Dramatist*, Elek, 1973.
Brimstone and Treacle (stage version), Methuen, 1978.
Pennies From Heaven, Quartet Books, 1981.
Waiting for the Boat, Faber and Faber, 1984.
Black Eyes (novel), Faber and Faber, 1987 (to be a four-part film series).
The Singing Detective, Faber and Faber, 1986.

SIMON RAVEN, *Royal Foundation & Other Plays* including *The Move Up Country*; *The Gaming Book*; *The Scapegoat*; *Sir Jocelyn – The Minister Would Like A Word*, Blond, 1966.

PHIL REDMOND, *Grange Hill Scripts*, Longman, 1985.

JACK ROSENTHAL, *Another Sunday and Sweet FA* in *The Television Dramatist*, Elek, 1973.
Bar Mitzvah Boy; *The Evacuees*; *Spend, Spend, Spend* in *Three Award Winning TV Plays*, Penguin, 1978.
Three Plays, Penguin, 1986.

DAVID RUDKIN, *Penda's Fen*, Davis-Poynter, 1975.

WILLY RUSSELL, *Break In* in *Scene Scripts Two*, Longman, 1978.
Our Day Out in *Act One*, Hutchinson, 1979.

JEREMY SANDFORD, *Cathy Come Home*, Calder and Boyars, 1976.
Edna, the Inebriate Woman, Calder and Boyars, 1976.

HOWARD SCHUMAN, *Censored Scenes from King Kong* in *Gambit Magazine*, 26/27, Calder and Boyars, 1975.

TOM STOPPARD, *A Separate Peace* (stage version) in *Playbill Two*, Hutchinson Educational, 1969.
Professional Foul in *Every Good Boy Deserves Favour & Professional Foul*, Faber and Faber, 1978.

MIKE STOTT, *Soldiers Talking, Cleanly*, Eyre Methuen, 1978.

PETER TERSON, *The Ballad of Ben Bagot* in *Scene Scripts Two*, Longman, 1978.

J. C. TREWIN (ed.), *Elizabeth R*, Elek, 1972.
The Six Wives of Henry VIII, Elek, 1972.

DAVID TURNER, *Way Off Beat* in *Conflicting Generations*, Longman, 1968.

EDMUND WARD, *The Challengers*, Elek, 1972.

FAY WELDON, *Polaris* in *Best Radio Plays*, Eyre Methuen, 1978.
Time Hurries On in *Scene*, Longman, 1972.

JULIE WELCH, *Singles* in *Sport*, Studio, 1980.

COLIN WELLAND, *Bank Holiday* in *Scene Scripts Two*, Longman, 1978.

JOHN WHITING, *A Walk in The Desert* in *Collected Plays*, Vol. 2, Heinemann Educational, 1969.

SNOO WILSON, *A Greenish Man* (stage version), Pluto Press, 1979.

Books on writing for television and film

MANUEL ALVAREDO and EDWARD BUSCOMBE, *Hazel: The Making of a TV Series*, BFI/Latimer, 1978.
A useful casebook of the studio production of a popular 'private eye' drama for Thames Television.

GEORGE W. BRANDT (ed.), *British Television Drama*, Cambridge University Press, 1981.
Essays on 'serious' television drama with chapters on the work of some major television writers, including Jeremy Sandford, Jim Allen, Trevor Griffiths and Dennis Potter.

BRIAN COOKE, *Writing Comedy for Television*, Methuen, 1983.

JOHN ELLIOT, *Mogul: The Making of a Myth*, Longman, 1973.

WILLIAM GOLDMAN, *Adventures in the Screen Trade*, Macdonald, 1984.
A personal view of Hollywood and screen writing.

STUART GRIFFITHS, *How Plays are Made*, Heinemann, 1982.
A methodical guide to the basic skills of writing television drama.

MALCOLM HULKE, *Writing for Television*, A. & C. Black, 1980.
Television writing techniques, production methods, how to develop plot and dialogue, script presentation.

MALCOLM HULKE and TERENCE DICKS, *The Making of 'Dr Who'*, Pan Books, 1972.

ALBERT HUNT, *The Language of Television – Uses and Abuses*, Methuen, 1983.

FRANK McCONNELL, *Storytelling and Mythmaking: Images from Film and Literature*, Oxford University Press, 1979.
Deals with literary forms and their scenic equivalents. McConnell provides his analysis of narrative archetypes divided into stages of development from the original epic myth to the modern ironic tone.

GERALD MILLERSON, *The Technique of TV Production*, Focal Press, 1985.
Deals with visual composition, the placing of characters in the frame, and discusses the use of height, size, lighting and colour for making different emphases.

BOB MILLINGTON and ROB NELSON, *The Boys from the Blackstuff – The Making of TV Drama*, Comedia/Routledge, 1986.

An academic's examination of the complete production process.

FRANK PIKE (ed.), *Ah! Mischief: The Writer and Television*, Faber, 1982.
A range of writers' views on the institutional problems associated with working in television drama.

DAVID SELF, *Television Drama: An Introduction*, Macmillan, 1984.
Provides general background on the production process of British television drama.

IRENE SHUBIK, *Play for Today: The Evolution of Television Drama*, Davis-Poynter, 1975.
The doyen of script editors and producers provides insights into the making of television drama from a producer's point of view. Plays covered include a detailed account of Jeremy Sandford's *Edna, the Inebriate Woman*.

SHAUN SUTTON, *The Largest Theatre in the World*, BBC Publications, 1982.
A history of British television drama by the longest-serving Head of BBC Television Drama Group.

CECIL P. TAYLOR, *Making a Television Play*, Oriel Press, 1970.

JOHN RUSSELL TAYLOR, *Anatomy of a Television Play*, Weidenfeld and Nicolson, 1962.
Production diaries of two ABC Armchair Theatre plays produced by Sidney Newman in the premier days of the single play.

FAY WELDON, *Letters to Alice – on first reading Jane Austen*, Michael Joseph, 1984.
A revealing attempt at analysing the process of writing and the nature of story-telling.

FRANCIS WHEEN, *Television*, Century Publishing, 1985.
A book of the television series that provides the general reader with an outline survey of the development of television and its programme output in international terms.

Some reference books

BBC Annual Report and Accounts From BBC Books.

BFI Film and Television Handbook Free to BFI full members; from BFI Publications.

Broadcast Production Guide From Broadcast.
The list includes small independent companies.

Contacts From Spotlight.

IBA Annual Report and Accounts From HMSO.
(Has charts of programmes made and comments on ITV companies and Channel 4.)

The Screen Writer's Guide, Zoetrope, 838 Broadway, New York, NY 10003, USA.
The handbook for film and television sales.

The TV Directory From Hamilton House Publishing.

The Writers' Handbook, ed. Barry Turner, Papermac, 1989.
Covers all markets including radio, film and television scripts and documentaries plus other literary outlets.

Writers' and Artists' Year Book, A. & C. Black.
Contains a lot of general information as well as lists of agents, publishers and a section on broadcasting.

Part 2

Introduction to the Plays

Hilary Salmon

In a big national drama competition the producer's fear is usually: will we find anything good enough to make? *Debut on Two* had the added constraint of looking for writers who hadn't written for the screen before. And yet we had no problem in drawing up an excellent short list which was in strong competition with the finalists. The *Debut on Two* book is a unique opportunity to see eight plays in print which have taken up the fifteen-minute challenge and looked again at the meaning of structure, character, location and language.

In looking through the commissioned plays some will seem more 'fantastic' than others, with perhaps *You Lucky Swines* and its shocking authenticity standing at one end of the spectrum and *Skin* with its entirely imaginary world at the other. But a close analysis will show that each of the plays chips and sometimes shatters the naturalistic mould that has shaped the television play for so long.

In imitating everyday life naturalism uses several conventions and you only have to break one of them to find a new illumination or give a necessary jolt. *The Wake*, *A Box of Swan* and *Skin* all use flashback (breaking the convention of consecutive time) to show how memory affects and is affected by the present. In *The Wake*, waiting for Tommy in the present triggers memories for Frances of waiting for Lucien in the past. As the betrayals of both men converge towards the end of the play we begin to see how Frances's own passivity has contributed to her impoverished series of relationships. *A Box of Swan* combines flashback with fantasy to show how John's mind daydreams in and out of reality in his attempt to reconcile his unhappy memories of his dead father. *Skin* also uses fantasy images, happily exploiting the possibilities of video, to underline its central metaphor for disability. The girl's invented disability in *Skin* is very carefully chosen: it enables the writer to speak for all disabilities, without generalising; by its seasonal impact it shows how an able-bodied person can be suddenly and drastically debilitated; and by affecting every part of the external surface of the girl's body it can look at the extent to which the person inside is dominated by her condition.

In *Poppylands*, Wayne dares to comment: 'I'm beginning to think that this is the end for naturalistic dialogue'; and certainly, in creating a language for the future, the play stretches the boundaries of everyday speech (without ever, by the way, using a word that doesn't yet exist). Less obviously, *The Wake* and *Window of Vulnerability* both use monologue which, although a dramatic convention of good pedigree, is not naturalism. If we saw Esther and Ruth in the interview which is at the heart of *Window of Vulnerability* would the writer achieve as much with equal economy and depth? Probably not in fifteen minutes anyway. *Breast is Best* also employs a kind of monologue; characters talk at rather than to the mute Server who is, for most of the play, represented by the camera's point of view. These strong comic diatribes from the Mother, the Customer, the Manager and the Photographer are written in a heightened or larger-than-life style which underlines the weakness of the Server's position. Should she support her friend and lose her job, or obey the Manager and uphold Society's hypocritical and contradictory attitudes to the female body? *You Lucky Swines* similarly uses heightened comic dialogue to illuminate the resigned and ironic response of the women to their own impotence. Finally, in one wordless and impossible act, the central character in *The Conversion of St Paul* turns the play on its head with the only strength he has: the power of his vocal chords.

How can a play that lasts fifteen minutes take on content of any real weight? None of the plays selected for *Debut on Two* would have been chosen if the content – what they had to say – hadn't been original, interesting and expressed with conviction. Few overtly political plays of any merit came through from our readers; instead, writers concentrated on getting character and location right and used very specific, often very personal short stories to illuminate larger political or social, the so-called public, issues. Often the point of view of the play is one which automatically challenges the perspective of the world we live in. Six of the writers chose women as the motivating forces of their plays. The tragi-comic world of working-class Liverpool in *You Lucky Swines* is distinguished from the world of *Boys from the Blackstuff* precisely because it is seen through the women's eyes. *The Wake* is eloquent about the way some women perceive themselves in relation to men, the way men oppress them and women oppress each other without ever referring even obliquely to feminism as an issue. Emily, in *Poppylands*, is searching for the greatest message of all in a world where humanity has no hope of a future. She is attracted by the violence of her world and appalled by it; she is free and unfree. And because she is interesting we follow her on her journey to Sheringham and back and imagine we have seen the mud flats and the horrible baptisms of the Shannocks, although we've never left Poppylands café. Esther has a similar horrifying journey across the estate in *Window of Vulnerability*. Again, because she describes the event with such pain and clarity, we imagine we have seen through her window into the world outside. In *Skin*, which is essentially a love story constrained by disability, the Girl realises that the Boy's love is impaired because he can never finally be her and that her love for him is frozen by the overwhelming fact of her physical condition. A play about the 'issue' of disability which could almost be mistaken for a poignant teenage romance.

Four of the plays, including *Poppylands* and *Window of Vulnerability*, deal with physical violence and the desire to escape from it (even Emily chooses a quiet life after shooting Mitch in *Poppylands*). The sensitive trumpeter's wish is fulfilled as he escapes south from violent, macho Dundee in *The Conversion of St Paul*. The combination of visual imagery of this piece with its significant interlocking road bridges and waterways and soaring jazz soundtrack is very potent. In *You Lucky Swines*, Martha has already escaped in her own way a male-dominated society but the play carefully acknowledges the personal price she has to pay.

The scripts that are published here are final drafts as they existed before the production process got under way. Since then the director, actors and pressures of time and money will all have altered and honed the writer's vision and it will be a useful learning exercise to compare the scripts here with the transmitted plays. Ultimately the only real interface between the writer and the audience is the event of the pre-recorded play 'going out'. As the *Debut on Two* plays go out, the writers will be asking audiences to use not just their eyes, ears and intellects but their dreams and imaginations too.

Skin

Nicola Batty

SCENE 1

A blank screen, flesh-coloured. Slowly appears the vague outline of a naked human figure; it is glittering and moving like a heat-sensitive photo. There is faint music, the discordant jangling of bells, like ice against ice, growing louder. Voice over of Narrator: slow and languid, as if in a trance. The music halts abruptly.

NARRATOR (*Voice over.*) Sometimes I seem to be changing like a chameleon. One moment my skin is white;

The figure turns white.

almost transparent with cold;

The figure turns transparent; camera moves closer to hands, which the figure holds out before it, as if in supplication.

then my fingers turn raw and sore;

The hands are turning redder as the figure turns side on.

but I know that my feet inside my boots are beginning to glow

Camera shifts from hands, down body, which is turning pink, then white, to feet.

just a faint subtle hint of blue.

The feet are blue. The jangling grows louder as the blue becomes clearer, sharper. Abruptly the bells stop as the blue becomes sky, clear and icy. Silence. The camera moves slowly down over the treetops, which are bare. It is winter, a small suburban park with a couple of benches surrounding a circular patch of bare earth, which in the summer is a rosebed. Camera pulls out to reveal Narrator sitting on bench, staring ahead, without emotion or movement. He is a young man in his early twenties, with short, cropped hair, wearing jeans, baseball boots and a short tartan 'lumberjack' jacket. It's cold, and his hands are buried in his pockets.

The voice over becomes ordinary and conversational.

It's sitting in this damned freezing park that does it.

Pause.

That, and the thought of you.

Camera moves slowly in on his face.

I accept the fact that you're gone, the cold got just too much for you, I suppose. But I won't accept the fact that you expect me to forget you, because I can't.

Camera moves closer, into his eyes, which are an icy blue-green. It becomes out of focus, and sparkling, like before.

The sparkling stuff comes into focus, gaining colour, and texture. It's a girl's hair; a long, dishevelled mass of silver hair. She turns. She is looking down; she could be asleep. As her face becomes clearer, she looks up suddenly; her eyes are a bright green.

I remember you. I remember your hair. It was the most amazing stuff. Silver like when the lights are full on at Stockport County.

The Girl's face breaks into a smile. The camera pulls back to reveal her walking along a busy shopping street. She wears black jeans and jumper over her thin, fragile-looking body. Passers-by occasionally stare or point at her hair, but she ignores them, looking in shop-windows, and sometimes smiling to herself.

Everyone stared when she walked by, this silver hair like tinsel down her back, and it glowed in the dark.

The Girl stops as it grows dark behind her.

I could hold my watch up near her face and tell the time accurately in the dark. I could never forget her hair, you know.

*As she stands, with her face uplifted, she is bathed in moonlight. She
closes her eyes and basks in its glow.*

GIRL (*Voice over.*) The sensation of the light falling on my face was more
real to me than I was to him.

Camera moves up and in on moon, full and bright.

He thought that he could share whatever I felt . . . but the cold
could not touch him.

Scene 2
Still on the moon. It slowly dissolves into an egg shape.

GIRL (*Voice over.*) He only saw my skin which was smooth and white. My
body, unblemished; round and smooth, like an egg.

*There is a tapping noise coming from within the egg, which shakes
as it grows clearer, gently at first, then more violently.*

Perhaps he's afraid that one day I will crack open,

The egg cracks; the tapping stops.

and a rough-skinned urchin will climb from my epidermis,

*A dark-haired girl wearing a crinkled lizard skin climbs from the
shell, kicks the two broken halves away, and stands face on, her
hands on her hips.*

and real life will pull through once again.

*The camera pulls back from the lizard woman, until she is a tiny
figure on a poster for a film on the wall of Woolworth's.*

Sometimes I think that he simply conjured me up from his visions
of another time, another place.

*The camera pulls back further to reveal Narrator standing looking
at poster. Other shoppers pass. There is the hubbub of voices; a baby
crying.*

NARRATOR (*Voice over.*) But when I was with her, I swelled visibly with
pride.

*He turns. She is behind him; she leads him away, talking. They
thread their way through the crowds.*

When we walked through Woolworth's people turned and whispered. She was indifferent to them.

They stop as she searches through a tray of combs.

She searched through the plastic combs trying to find a silver one with which to comb her beautiful hair.

She finds one and holds it up. The camera moves in on it, and it glitters like ice. It blurs, out of focus. Slowly the teeth disintegrate and fall to the ground like drops of water.

When she got home, she removed all of the teeth, saying that they got caught in her hair and brought tears to her eyes.

SCENE 3
The droplets of water slow as they fall to the ground, blur, become leaves. Autumn leaves fluttering gently to the ground. The camera pulls back to reveal the Girl sweeping up fallen leaves in a garden; while the Narrator leans against a fence or the side of the house, watching her.

GIRL Don't you love the atmosphere of autumn?
NARRATOR (*Voice over.*) She would say as the air grew colder . . .

She stops sweeping and the camera moves in slowly on her.

GIRL There is a chill edge to the woodsmoke . . . and it slices you like a razor.

Her smile fades as the camera moves in on her face, and she closes her eyes. A tear slips from beneath her eyelashes and we follow it down her face.

NARRATOR (*Voice over.*) And she would wince as though the air really were sharp.

The tear falls, slowly. It shatters like glass as it hits the ground.

Her silver tears would splash on to the dead leaves like crystal.

The camera returns to her face, moving closer. She bleeds in places.

When winter came she would bleed . . . raw cuts appeared on her face and hands like splashes of tomato sauce, and she would shake her head and turn away so that I couldn't see them.

*She turns quickly back. She has stopped bleeding; as the camera
pulls back, she laughs.*

When spring came I would feel a great relief wash over and she
would laugh once again.

SCENE 4

*The camera pulls out; her smile fades as we see that she is sitting on
the bench in the park. The Narrator sits beside her, staring ahead,
motionless. She is half turned towards him, and looking at him,
though he will not look at her.*

NARRATOR (*Voice over.*) It was in this very same spot that I'm sitting in
now, two months ago, it must be, that she took my hand and told
me that she was leaving.

She takes his hand and speaks.

GIRL It's something I need, I have to do. Please try and understand. I
have to leave now . . . while I still have control.

*The Narrator stares ahead, making no response. But his voice over
is soft and shaken.*

NARRATOR (*Voice over.*) Her hair glittered like incandescent moon-
beams in the semi-darkness.

GIRL You don't have to stay around because you feel sorry for me or anything.

Pause.

Please try and understand. There are no chains, you know.

Pause.

It's my skin . . . you see only my skin, although there is more to me
than that.

*She drops her eyes to their hands, her hand on his. The camera
moves in on their hands.*

NARRATOR (*Voice over.*) I sat there for a long time, with her hand gripping mine. I felt – well, I don't know – numb, I suppose, like I was
dead or at least in suspended animation.

He raises his hand, the fingers spread. As the camera moves in on it
it becomes, slowly, a leaf.

I could almost hear the leaves tumbling around us. It was autumn
again.

The leaf turns red, gold; it begins to shrivel up and disintegrate.

From then on it was always autumn. Dying. Everything was always
in a state of decay or disintegration and me, as well. And her. Us.

The camera leaves the decomposed leaf and moves up, to their hands
gripping each other. Camera moves out; they sit, as before, on the
bench. They don't look at each other; she looks down, at their hands,
and he stares ahead.

I can still feel her hand gripping mine.

The camera moves in on her face.

Already her skin was beginning to tear in places and blood oozed
through the cracks.

Closer on her skin. A trickle of blood travels slowly over the surface.
The camera follows it down.

I wondered how she managed to wash herself.

Her skin, and the trickle of blood, meet water. Then runs into the
water, forming cloudy patterns. As the camera pulls back, we see
that the Girl is sitting in the bath, with her back towards us.

I could imagine her scrubbing her back with that long-handled
brush – the one with the mushrooms painted on the pale blue surface – that my mum gave her last Christmas,

She scrubs her back; she hums and there are usual bath-time
sounds.

and the stiff bristles ripping right through her white skin, slicing
right the way down her back,

As the camera moves in on the water below her back, all the sounds
cease slowly.

making a deep trench like an open mouth which would gape stu-
pidly at the shiny chrome bathtaps.

Drip, drip, drip. Blood falls in the water, faster and faster.

The blood fills my mind even as I imagine until it blinds me. It has blinded me to anything she may feel or think . . .

SCENE 5

The camera moves in on the patterns the blood makes in the water. It blurs, and when it comes back into focus it's the patterns on the Narrator's red lumberjacket. The camera pulls back to reveal him sitting on the bench in the park as before. It's winter, freezing cold. He looks up and around suddenly, as though for rain.

NARRATOR (*Voice over.*) I look up, imagining that I see snowflakes fall-ing around me, but it is too cold for that. Sometime, I can't say exactly when, autumn turned to winter. The temperature dropped still further.

He stands slowly and turns to his right.

She couldn't bear it. Last time I saw her she was crying;

She moves into view, standing close to him. They look at each other; she is crying and bleeding.

the tears mingling with the blood on her cheeks.

GIRL I can't stay here any longer. I can't. This is all becoming too real.

NARRATOR (*Voice over.*) She told me, turning away as I reached out to wipe the blood from her eyes.

She drops her eyes, turning and walking slowly away from him.

GIRL You think that it's my skin . . . but it's not. You see, I don't feel anything any more. I have become so cold . . . so very cold.

She walks out of shot. The camera moves in on Narrator, who stands, expressionless, and stares after her.

NARRATOR (*Voice over.*) I bury my hands further into the pockets of my jacket as the cold begins to get to me.

The camera moves in on his face as, faintly, the bells begin to jangle discordantly.

The air is as sharp and as vicious as a knife; I can feel it trying to cut right through my skin,

The camera moves closer and closer in on his skin, showing the creases and marks in it.

but, you know, my skin is just too tough.

Closer. The bells get louder and louder. Then abruptly they stop, and there is a total blackout.

The End.

Poppylands

Paul Cornell

SCENE 1. EXTERIOR. STOCK FOOTAGE. DAY.
Stock footage of waves breaking on a cold shore.
Music: Debussy's 'Cathedral Under the Sea'.
Fade into Emily's speech, which is a voice over.

EMILY (*Voice over.*) Geography. That's what happens when you give a country over to ice water. New things are made. I paid a bargewoman with milk to get me to Cromer. She didn't say anything.

SCENE 2. INTERIOR. SNACK BAR. DAY.
An old place, chipped laminate tables, milk ads from the sixties, grime in crevices. A glass-top bar with a range of sandwiches, ancient menus. Sitting at a table are Keef, the owner, middle-aged, in an apron, and Wayne, an older man. Wayne is asking Keef questions out of a gaudy booklet labelled 'Crusty Old Innkeeper'.

WAYNE A stranger enters your bar. What is your greeting, Keef?
KEEF Arr, t'aint no fit day for man nor beast. Come in out of the cold and warm yerself. Jug of ale?
WAYNE Well, yes, just about. Are you supposed to embellish?
KEEF That be all part of it, Wayne. I paid a goodly penny for me role. Don't want to let 'em down.

The door opens. Enter Emily, a teenager in leather jacket and mirrorshades. Keef stands up.

KEEF Arr, t'aint no fit day for man nor beast, come –

EMILY In out of the cold? Really got any ale, have you?

KEEF No.

EMILY Then coffee, heavy caffeine. And not a word more of that stereotyper shit.

> *Angry, but silent, Keef goes to brew up. Emily sits by Wayne.*

EMILY Knew another crusty innkeeper in Norwich. Broke his finger one night.

WAYNE A child, in here. She is rude to Keef.

EMILY Oh, Christ!   *She swigs from hip flask.*

Are you all rotted, or what? Who's going to introduce us here? I'll do it. I'm Emily, from Norwich. Took a week to get here by barge, and I'm armed. Etiquette intact?

WAYNE Yeh. I'm Wayne, from here, took me three minutes by walking. I'm listening to you.

EMILY Aren't you a traditionalist? Well, I'm the kind who talks in all the wrong places. Your lot would say I watch too many old videos. Your lot. 'Sides, what do we talk about, the weather?

> *Wayne chuckles politely. This irritates Emily even more.*

WAYNE Why are you here? There's not much in Poppylands for your age.

EMILY You should see Norwich. Full of stereotypers. I mean, what's happening? So few people about, you got to be recognised, or what? Out-in-the-cold . . .

WAYNE We're a conservative little community. I'm afraid the big firms get many requests for roles from us.

> *Keef brings coffee and tea over.*

KEEF Summat to do.

EMILY Not even true Anglia, is it?

> *Keef goes off to water his plant, the only one in the bar.*

WAYNE Does it have to be?

EMILY Your game, your rules. I'm not interested in the world's spillings. I've been playing your arcades this morning, and they don't kill me well.

WAYNE So why are you here?

EMILY I'm here for the religion, Wayne. I'm only the first. Word is that the real thing's happening over in Sheringham.

KEEF Wouldn't go there. Bad smell comes along the coast now.

EMILY You won't, I will. Tomorrow, if I can find a bed tonight. Need warmth, Wayne?

WAYNE Perhaps, but I think I'm too old. I don't feel much now. Are you going to walk across the waters with one of the Christian parades?

Emily pours a drop from her flask into Wayne's tea.

EMILY No. Here, try it. Perhaps I can get you drunk and use your bed. No, I'm going on my own. I want to see a living Shannock, and then see a Christian parade kill him. That's real reality for you, not all this endless water.

WAYNE Blood, yes, of course. Your amusements are harsher now. Are the pirates still going strong?

KEEF Ha! You 'aven't listened to 'em for years, Wayne! All of 'em just talk about God on the waves now, and play cut-up screechin's.

EMILY Yeah? Well, most things are better when they've been cut up. You ever broke a stylus on the vinyl? Can't do that with a laser. You ever play something down to a bunch of fuzzy knives?

She throws back a gulp from the flask and stares at them, as if unsure where she is.

WAYNE Well . . . perhaps . . .

EMILY No! I don't care about length and meter! Don't care! This world's gonna be gone under waves of rhythm in a couple of years and I'm gonna cut it up while I can.

WAYNE You really have been seeing too many old videos. The world might survive a bit longer without all this violence.

EMILY And that's harsh criticism from you, isn't it? I've been watching too much reality!

She stands up to go.

No fun. Mother had a guy used to put money in her mouth. Wouldn't mind money, but there's none left to gag on. You're talking nothing and you're going to die. Bye.

Wayne shakes his head as she leaves.

WAYNE Between you and her, Keef, I'm beginning to think that this is the end for naturalistic dialogue.

KEEF Didn't even 'ave an egg for me.

WAYNE What's she after? Isn't living enough?

KEEF T'aint for us to say, is it?

WAYNE I wish you'd stop doing that for a while, Keef, I really do.

Outside the graffiti-scrawled window, there is movement. A brush slaps across it with a whack of tar.

SCENE 3. EXTERIOR. SNACK BAR. DAY.
We can see that the place is called 'Poppylands'. Emily is watching Mitch, a young man in a survival suit and scarf, paint a tar Christ on to the window.

EMILY Why is it like that?

MITCH It's Christ, badly hurt, really suffering, waiting to come again in new flesh.

EMILY I know how that feels.

He takes a spray can and uses it sparingly to scrawl a cross over the picture.

Oh. Bad.

MITCH I try not to be. What difference can this make now, when you think about it? We're waiting for a sort of ultraviolet passover. We're marking all the buildings so God won't hurt them with hard radiation.

EMILY That's the costume, too?

MITCH Partly. I'm going over to Sheringham this afternoon on a parade. Some really odd people are going about their business there, and we have to give the place a better image, ready for the Lord.

EMILY I want to go.

MITCH Do you know God?

EMILY Well, yeh, I'm not into the belief yet. I just want to watch.

MITCH That's a start. It's a good experience, it could make you want to know more, and I hope so. You haven't much time left, you know. Follow me.

EMILY Okay . . .

SCENE 4. EXTERIOR. STOCK FOOTAGE. NIGHT.
Stock footage of a raging sea crashing on a beach, and a full moon.
Silence except for Emily's voice over.

EMILY (*Voice over.*) Have you ever gripped the hands of a chair and bit your tongue to the music? The music is what people call communication, and that's so much shit, because we're alone in our minds with every piece.

A performer might reach out and say he loves you, but you know that's only him with his concepts. A Christ might really love you all, so no wonder he's wounded, so many minds biting his. They called Anglia Poppylands, like it really was covered in flowers. That's that kind of soft lie, it makes people feel that love's written into the world. The world comes tumbling down, but the people won't come with it. They just put their hands in their laps and say how bad it is. Censor me, addict me, put me to work and make me angry. Maybe they'll just make you too tired to dream.

Well, let me tell you: the gap between people is forever and ever, and death is death, and if you can fool yourself into feeling with a Shannock's blood on you, and a Christian crossing himself between your thighs, then who's to say that's anywhere near wrong?

Emily's face superimposed on to the waves.

And all it came down to was being alone with someone inside you, bayonet or tongue or penis. I ate a Christian and left him weeping into the sand, 'cos he'd lost a place in the Great Godfuck that was heading up for him like a brick wall. Sing heaven for me, children.

Blackness.

SCENE 5. INTERIOR. SNACK BAR. DAY.
The next morning. Enter Wayne, shaking his umbrella. Keef is watering his plant.

WAYNE Good Lord, Keef, it gets worse every day.
KEEF Bad walk, was it?
WAYNE Muddier than usual. I wonder if Emily got to Sheringham?
KEEF Reckon she did. Different to us, them young 'uns.

Wayne sits down, Keef brings him his usual tea.

WAYNE Are they? It seems to me that it's everything we ever did, played at full volume. People are people . . .

KEEF Unless they be Shannocks! Foul things, they weren't around then.

WAYNE Is that you or the Innkeeper?

KEEF There be no room at this inn for the likes of them!

WAYNE You know, Keef, the Neanderthals and *Homo sapiens* lived together on this coast for about six thousand years. We didn't breed meanly then. Why can't the young live with the Shannocks?

KEEF Who'd want to? Them with their blubber and smell. Polluted things.

WAYNE No, no . . . they're just the next generation, ready for the winter. I think there's the Word at work, you know, order out of chaos. I think some of the young just want to be them, don't want to be left behind.

KEEF Left behind? It's them who's left us behind. We haven't taught 'em anything. They ain't got no civilisation.

WAYNE Humanity goes on without us, Keef. We haven't got to teach them anything that the wet and the cold haven't already. The Shannocks will win out in the end, and they'll keep humanity going for a while, wars and religions and all.

KEEF You a Christian then, Wayne?

WAYNE I was, but it left me behind. I get the feeling that Christ had better come soon, or he'll be in a different image this time.

KEEF Wayne . . .

Keef pulls up his sleeve to show his upper arm. It is covered in fatty bulges, sprouting hard black hairs.

WAYNE Well, well, old friend. A Shannock in Cromer.

KEEF All my limbs are like this. Since I was fifteen. I never told anybody.

WAYNE Don't worry. You're one of the chosen few now, Keef. Just don't let the mob see it.

KEEF I don't dare go near salt water, this is made for the inland seas. Salt makes me peel. That's what the smell from Sheringham is . . .

Emily enters. Wayne shields Keef as he pulls his sleeve down.

EMILY I went to Sheringham.

WAYNE And what was it like?

They sit down.

EMILY Not exciting, but dirty. No Christ down there, but they keep looking.

KEEF Looking?

EMILY Yeh. They're baptising them in the sea, all the Shannocks. When one floats and doesn't scald he gets to be Jesus. Know what?

WAYNE No.

EMILY He isn't coming.

WAYNE Oh.

EMILY I went over there expecting a nice edge, y'know, ripping up the town. Drama, religion, the end of the world. And it was just a bunch of people going through the old-fashioned motions. Is this Jesus? Splash, fizz, no. Is this Jesus? Splash, fizz, no . . . I mean, man, violence is me, but torture is just civilisation all over. Old world never hit a guy till they were really down.

KEEF How many were there?

EMILY Lots. They either run inland or line up for a swim. You know, if he does arrive, he'll be up for the crucifixion before he can say anything . . .

WAYNE Maybe that's the idea. So was the day a total loss?

EMILY I had a Christian, but he was so hung up about disease and sin and punishment that I nearly had to rape him. Christ, what else is there to do?

WAYNE If I said 'How about painting a picture with me?' what would you do?

EMILY I'd bare my teeth and enjoy it. Where are the cans?

WAYNE No, my sort of picture. Oils at home.

EMILY You good? If you are, I'm not interested.

WAYNE I've never done it before. I found the materials on a dump. Nobody was interested enough to destroy them.

EMILY Yeh.

They get up to leave. A flat skipping stone smashes through the tarred window.

KEEF Wayne!

The door bursts open, revealing Mitch carrying a bucket of water.

MITCH Emily! I want you to face up to the Lord for what you've done.

EMILY Mitch, I –

MITCH I've been forgiven, but I have to try to save you too. All you have to do is let his love into your heart, and ask for mercy –

Emily gets up and stands close to Mitch.

EMILY Mercy for what?

MITCH For . . . me. You preyed on me.

EMILY You used me for prayer. You were calling out to Mother Mary when you came.

MITCH I've sinned, yes. I want you to see your sin too, and accept this water if you're pure – and please God let you be pure . . .

EMILY Pure?! Oh no . . . you think? –

Emily grabs Mitch by the collar and kisses him violently. He is afraid, and tries to throw the water over her, but she uses her embrace to struggle, and they totter about the room, Emily laughing, Mitch praying out loud.

MITCH Oh God, spare me from contamination, make me clean, keep me fresh . . .

EMILY Maybe sorry, that's all you get, Mitch. Now I gotta go, I have to paint.

Wayne has been getting between Keef and the bucket, but now he comes forward to try and intercede.

WAYNE Excuse me –

Mitch wrests the bucket from Emily and throws the seawater over her. She only gets wet, but a splash hits Keef's arm. He squeals and pulls up the cloth to reveal a scalded mass of blubber. Mitch notices. He reaches for his bucket.

WAYNE Keef! Jesus!

MITCH Death! Destroy it all!

EMILY So you finally got the idea? Too late.

She knees him in the groin, he crumples. Wayne has rushed to help Keef.

EMILY Get him outside, bathe it in muddy water!

WAYNE Emily . . .

EMILY D'you think I care? Go on!

Wayne helps Keef out of the door. Emily produces a handgun from her jacket.

MITCH Emily . . . what?

EMILY Playing, only playing. We're all just second-hand goods now.

She gently props his head up against the table, and nuzzles the gun to his forehead.

EMILY Submit?

He nods, dumbly anaesthetised.

That's all right, then. It's all right.

She shoots him through the head.

SCENE 6. INTERIOR. SNACK BAR. DAY.

A splash of red that Emily has just slapped on the canvas to the sound of a gunshot carried over from the previous scene. Wayne is beside her, and responds with a green line under the splash. Keef, his arm in a sling, is watering his plants, a great many of them now, covering the walls. There are also books and a record player which is playing the Jesus and Mary Chain's 'In a Hole' softly. The bar is no longer in business. Emily's speech is a voice over.

EMILY (*Voice over.*) It's good to die knowing you're right, I suppose. You can only really heal people after they're dead. Poppylands had become a home, and after we went, it would become something old in the sand for people to talk about in the vast sweep of different history in front of us. Keef didn't mind. He was going to migrate soon, to join the new flesh. Wayne and me, we were going to do paintings and books, and bury them. Send some fun to the future.

Keef says that there's a different smell on the breeze now, and sometimes he hears the calls of new humanity when the wind comes from the west.

Keef opens a window and begins to wipe some of the graffiti off.

We've got time now, without having to run about after anything. I hope I get old before I die. Right now, there's plenty of time for the game.

The End.

You Lucky Swines

Shaun Duggan

CAST

Martha Whitter Mid-thirties. Mother to Janice and ex-wife of Brian. Still loves Brian but not his drink. More ambitious than the others.

Bill Whitter Father to Martha, Pauline, Eileen and others. Drunk, thin, wrinkled pensioner – normally senile. Hates Martha for divorcing 'perfect' husband Brian.

Brian Late thirties. Drunk, simply follows the patterns a male should. Loves and misses Martha but prefers his drink.

Winnie Whitter Wife to Bill. Too easy-going. Fat, grey perm and thick glasses. Simply wants a quiet life. Sadly doesn't get it.

Janice Aged fifteen. Daughter of Martha and Brian. Also a chain-smoker. Had a dreadfully painful youth. On the look-out for her ideal man – a strong butcher or bricklayer.

Kate Host of reception. Mother to Marty (Winnie's son-in-law). Mid-sixties, simple sense of humour.

Pauline Early twenties. Mother of Jennifer Ringo and Thomas George – expecting another. Accepts her role in life as a baby machine and enjoys the domestic problems of labour and a strained marriage.

Marty Mid-twenties. Husband to Pauline. Fat, balding, ugly and toothless.

SCENE 1. INTERIOR. MARTHA'S HOUSE: LIVING ROOM. DAY.
Martha sits sprawled reading the Sunday papers while drinking a
mug of tea. Janice rushes about.

JANICE Why didn't you get me up?

MARTHA I didn't think. I thought you were up anyway.

JANICE Why aren't you coming?

MARTHA Because he'll be there.

JANICE Who, me dad?

MARTHA Yes, and your grandad too. Then again that depends on what type of mood he's in.

JANICE Look at the state of me hair.

MARTHA Anyway, even if he does go he'll only make a show of Pauline and argue with somebody.

JANICE I promised our Eileen I'd mind Barry, Damon, Scott and little Kylie today too. She fancies the vicar and doesn't want him to know she's got kids. It'll be dead good today, it'll be like having four kids of me own.

MARTHA Some people just don't want to learn. Is it in St Matthews?

JANICE No, it's in that little church in Croxteth.

MARTHA How come?

JANICE Don't you ever listen?

MARTHA (*To herself.*) I try not to.

JANICE Because Marty's a Protestant and he *insists* the kids are too.

MARTHA Our Pauline should put her foot down; Protestant churches are always horrible. Poor kids, like bloody mongrels.

JANICE Have you seen the other brush?

MARTHA You're not wearing that dress are you?

JANICE No, you're seeing things.

MARTHA Very funny. You know I don't like that dress on you.

JANICE Well there's loads of things of yours I don't like but I wouldn't tell you.

MARTHA (*Worried.*) What like?

JANICE Everything.

She smiles.

Oh God, I'm gonna be dead late.

SCENE 2. EXTERIOR. INTERIOR: TAXI. DAY.
We hear the sound of church bells ringing. A taxi is seen speeding through the crumbling housing estate. Inside the taxi are Winnie and Janice with seven young children.

JANICE I'm going mad I missed it. I could scream.

WINNIE You'll be able to see the photos. Our Kevin took some lovely ones – colour too.

JANICE Oh, that's good.

WINNIE Pauline was getting really annoyed, the vicar kept thinking Jennifer Ringo was a boy.

JANICE You're joking. Is that the one our Eileen fancies?

WINNIE No, she fancies the younger one. This one was the old feller – the one I fancy.

JANICE Oh, Nana!

They laugh.

SCENE 3. INTERIOR. TAXI. DAY.
The taxi is now stationary outside Kate's house. Inside are Winnie and Janice holding seven young children. Winnie is flustered and searching her handbag.

JANICE Here you are, Nana, another 20p.

WINNIE Right that's £1.60. We need another 30p.

JANICE Hang on, I'll run in and scav it off Pauline.

WINNIE Hurry up Janice . . .

To the taxi driver.

. . . She'll only be a sec. We're not usually like this but it's me grand-daughter's christening and our Pauline needed to lend money for a christening gown. I'll be all right tomorrow, I get me pension.

Winnie sits embarrassed.

SCENE 4. EXTERIOR. KATE'S HOUSE: FRONT GARDEN. DAY.
Janice with four kids runs up the path. The garden is full of hundreds of abandoned babies and toddlers. Janice dumps hers on the grass – including little Kylie who can't walk. She goes into the house.

SCENE 5. INTERIOR. KATE'S HOUSE: LIVING ROOM. DAY.
*The house is full of women mainly familiar to Janice. She says her
hellos.*

KATE Iyah, girl, how are you, Queen? Where's your Grandma?
JANICE She's in the taxi. Where's Pauline?
KATE She's through there with the now baptised Jennifer Ringo.

Laughs loudly.

SCENE 6. EXTERIOR. KATE'S HOUSE: FRONT GARDEN. DAY.
Kate passes the children and walks down the path to the taxi.

KATE Hello, Mrs Whitter. Are you staying in that taxi all day or coming
in?

Kate laughs hysterically.

WINNIE Iyah, Kate. No, I'm coming in now.
KATE I believe the christening was beautiful.
WINNIE Yes, little Jennifer Ringo didn't cry once.
KATE Oh, she's gorgeous isn't she?

Janice comes out and passes the money to Winnie.

WINNIE Thank you.

*They all begin to walk up the path. Music coming from the house is
loud.*

KATE This do is gonna be great. I'm on the look-out for a new feller.
Someone under thirty preferably with a big wallet.

They all laugh.

SCENE 7. INTERIOR. MARTHA'S HOUSE: LIVING ROOM. DAY.
*Martha is sat in front of the TV. The fire is on, the house is like a
pigsty but she doesn't care, she's quite content. She's got a nice hot
mug of tea and a box of Kleenex to her side.*

TV ANNOUNCER And here's the Sunday matinee for today. It's Hayley
Mills in *Whistle Down the Wind*.

*The music begins and Martha already has tears streaming down
her face.*

SCENE 8. INTERIOR. KATE'S HOUSE: LIVING ROOM. DAY.
*The living room is now full of women – no men. There is a spread of
food at one side. Music and lots of noise can be heard coming from
the next room.*

KATE Mrs Whitter, would you like some more trifle?

WINNIE (*With cream around her lips.*) Oh, yes please, Kate, that would be
lovely.

PAULINE Where's Marty gone?

KATE (*Proudly.*) Is there any need to ask? He's over in the Broady pub
with the rest of the lads. Your dad's over there, Janice love. They'll
all be over in a minute. Why didn't Bill come, Mrs Whitter?

WINNIE Is there any need to ask, Kate? He's sitting in, sulking.

KATE What's up with him? It's always people that have everything that
are always the most miserable, isn't it?

PAULINE Let's not talk about my dad. I don't want to spoil the day.

WINNIE You won't believe it, Kate. When it's my birthday he gets that
jealous he sulks all day. Our Martha hates him, ooh the rows that
they've had. She won't visit me anymore and she only rings when
she knows he'll be in the pub.

PAULINE (*Patting her inflated stomach.*) When he comes along, I'll get
him christened in the same church. I really enjoyed it today. I felt
dead important standing at the altar like the Pope or something.

KATE Have you got any names planned yet?

PAULINE Probably Jason Paul or Brian John.

Janice lights up a cigarette.

JANICE Christ, I've got school tomorrow. I can't stand it.

PAULINE You should do what Eileen did and get pregnant. You get
loads of time off.

JANICE I might wait until I'm in the fifth year.

PAULINE Get yourself a tall prefect.

JANICE Get lost! Prefects are always mongs. I want a bricky or something. You're dead lucky having Marty.

SCENE 9. INTERIOR. KATE'S HOUSE: LIVING ROOM. NIGHT.
*The front room is now full of drunk men too. We drop in on a few
conversations.*

BRIAN How's your mum?

JANICE She's all right.

BRIAN Is she working today?

JANICE No, she's off.

BRIAN Why didn't she come?

Pause.

Because I'm here?

JANICE (*Embarrassed.*) Yeah.

BRIAN (*Takes three pounds from his pocket.*) Here you are. I know you can't buy much with that.

JANICE Oh yirs! I'm saving up to hire a sunbed.

PAULINE (*Laughing.*) Look at my Marty, how many has he had now?

Marty is standing with a group of men arguing about football.
Kate begins to talk loudly to one of the toddlers.

KATE Thomas George, do you want another drink love?

The young boy nods his head.

Do you want milk love?

BOY I want beer.

Everyone roars with laughter.

MARTY Good lad, you'll be able to come to the pub with me soon, won't you son?

The innocent child nods excitedly.

KATE He'll be just like his dad when he's older!

MARTY I hope so.

Pauline looks proud. The boy goes over to Marty and begins to drink
beer from his glass. Everybody laughs.

WINNIE (*Stuffing a cream cake down her mouth and holding a baby.*) Are you coming to little Kylie's christening next week?

She points at the baby in her arms.

KATE Christ! Is it hers next week too?

WINNIE She's getting done in St Matthews and our Ei wants the do to be in ours.

KATE I bet you're looking forward to that, Mrs Whitter?

Laughs hysterically.

SCENE 10. INTERIOR. BILL'S HOUSE: BACK ROOM. NIGHT.
Bill is sitting in a miserable-looking living room. Curtains closed,
no lights. Just the glow from the coal fire. He puts down a bottle of
whisky. He gets up and walks out into the kitchen mumbling.

BILL Stupid bastard of a cow. She's out enjoying herself and I haven't eaten for thirteen days.

SCENE 11. INTERIOR. KATE'S HOUSE: LIVING ROOM. NIGHT.
Everyone has now left or is leaving. Children are asleep in every
known space. People are clearing up.

PAULINE What type of mood do you think he'll be in?
WINNIE It should be a good one if he's been drinking all day.

Janice excitedly runs to Winnie with the four kids.

JANICE Nana, Eileen's copped for the vicar, I said I'd take the kids back to yours for her. He's dead nice, he mentioned someone called Chris Dingle, it must be his mate, he said he comes around every year and he's invited me around, oh, he sounds dead nice. The vicar said something about him being festive and jolly. Oh, he sounds like a bricklayer!
KATE Have you had a nice time?
WINNIE Oh, Kate, it's been lovely, the best christening I've been to in weeks. The trifle was beautiful.
KATE Well, you seemed to be the only one who liked it, Mrs Whitter.
JANICE (*Holding baby.*) Don't forget it's hers next week.
KATE I won't, Queen. I'll see you then. Tarrah. Bye, little Kylie.

Kate sees them to the front door and waves them off down the street.

SCENE 12. EXTERIOR. BILL'S HOUSE: FRONT. NIGHT.
Winnie, Pauline, Janice and the six children approach the house.
They walk up the path.

WINNIE Don't knock, Pauline, I've got my key.
PAULINE All right, Mother, don't panic.
WINNIE Well, you know what he's like.

SCENE 13. INTERIOR. BILL'S HOUSE: BACK ROOM. NIGHT.
Bill hears the key in the door and shuffling in the hall.

SCENE 14. INTERIOR. BILL'S HOUSE: HALL/FRONT ROOM. NIGHT.
They sneak in the front room. Winnie puts on the gas fire.

PAULINE It's freezing in here.

WINNIE It warms up. I practically live in here now. Keep out of his way.

PAULINE Thank God I've got my own life. I wish he'd hurry up and die.

WINNIE Pauline! You don't mean that.

PAULINE I do, if he'd died years ago we'd all be happy now. Yeah! We should have all jumped on him and knifed him when we were kids.

WINNIE Isn't she terrible, Janice? .

Exits.

SCENE 15. INTERIOR. BILL'S HOUSE: BACK ROOM. NIGHT.
Winnie quietly opens the door and sneaks in. Bill's eyes are open but as Winnie sneaks around to see he closes them. She looks relieved and walks out.

SCENE 16. INTERIOR. BILL'S HOUSE: FRONT ROOM. NIGHT.
Winnie enters as Janice and Pauline are taking the chunky coats off the children.

WINNIE Oh, that's good, he's asleep. I'll go and put the kettle on.

SCENE 17. INTERIOR. MARTHA'S HOUSE: LIVING ROOM. NIGHT.
Martha is surrounded by screwed-up tissues and is drowning in tears. We watch the final scene of the film. The children look on as the criminal is searched. Hayley Mills says her final words. Titles and sad music. Martha is heart-broken. She blows her nose. Wipes her eyes and goes to the phone.

SCENE 18. INTERIOR. BILL'S HOUSE: FRONT ROOM. NIGHT.
The phone rings.

WINNIE (*Jumps up nervously.*) That'll be your mum, Janice.

SCENE 19. INTERIOR. BILL'S HOUSE: HALL. NIGHT.
Winnie goes into the hall and answers the phone.

WINNIE   Iyah, Martha. Yeah, it was lovely. I'm not whispering.

SCENE 20. INTERIOR. BILL'S HOUSE: BACK ROOM. NIGHT.
Bill is listening to their conversation.

WINNIE   (*Into phone.*) Yeah, the queer feller's in. But he's asleep, thank Christ.

SCENE 21. INTERIOR. MARTHA'S HOUSE: LIVING ROOM. NIGHT.

MARTHA   (*Into phone.*) Oh, I've had a lovely afternoon. I've done noth-ing but sit in and watch *Whistle Down the Wind.* Why didn't the queer feller go to the christening?

SCENE 22. INTERIOR. BILL'S HOUSE: BACK ROOM. NIGHT.
Bill is listening.

WINNIE   (*Out of vision.*) Oh you know how stupid he is. He would only have got jealous because he wasn't the centre of attention. Our Kathy phoned up yesterday and she was saying . . .

Bill gets up and goes into the hall.

SCENE 23. INTERIOR. BILL'S HOUSE: HALL/(INTERCUT) MARTHA'S HOUSE: LIVING ROOM. NIGHT.

BILL   Is that the other slag on the phone?
WINNIE   Yeah, he's just got up unfortunately. It's our Martha if you must know.
BILL   Give me that phone.

He snatches the phone. Shouting.

Listen you, ye' slag. I don't want you phoning up or coming any-where near this house again. You can piss off!

Slams down phone.

WINNIE   What did you do that for, you stupid get? I don't know what's up with you, she's done nothing to you. You're just bloody mental!

Bill goes back into his room slamming the door behind him, Winnie goes back into the front room. The phone rings again. Winnie runs out and answers it.

WINNIE Oh, hello, Martha, take no notice of him. He's puddled.
MARTHA (*Crying.*) Put him on, Mum.
WINNIE It's not worth the trouble.
MARTHA Stop defending him. I don't care how he treats you but he's not talking to me like that anymore.

Winnie puts the phone down to the side and goes to Bill's room.

WINNIE Our Martha wants you.
BILL (*Out of vision.*) I'm not going to speak to that slag.

Winnie goes back to the phone.

WINNIE No, he won't come, Martha, he's too bloody scared.
BILL (*Out of vision. Shouting.*) Am I shit!
WINNIE Our Martha says you either come to the phone now or she's coming down here to bleedin' murder you.

Bill runs into the hall and snatches the phone.

BILL Listen you, ye' whore. You're not coming anywhere near this house again. I don't want slags here so just piss off.

Slams phone down.

WINNIE You're puddled, bloody puddled. I wouldn't be surprised if our Martha is on her way around here now to kill you.

Bill slams the door again. Winnie goes back into the front room holding her head.

SCENE 24. *INTERIOR. BILL'S HOUSE: FRONT ROOM. NIGHT.*
Nervous silence.

PAULINE Do you think our Martha will come down?

Knowing pause.

I don't understand her. She had everything. Brian's great. She couldn't wish for anybody more normal. I'm going. I hate all these fights.

I'll take all the kids back round to Kate's for a few hours. Tell our Eileen I'll wash the christening gown for her – it's full of lager and she wants it for little Kylie next week.

WINNIE Janice, ring for a taxi, try and stop her.

SCENE 25. INTERIOR. MARTHA'S HOUSE: LIVING ROOM. NIGHT.
Martha is storming around the house crying. She is throwing on clothes.

SCENE 26. EXTERIOR. BILL'S HOUSE: TAXI. NIGHT.
Janice climbs into a taxi.

JANICE Stalisfield Avenue, quickly please.

SCENE 27. EXTERIOR. MARTHA'S HOUSE: TAXI. NIGHT.
Martha opens her front door and storms up the path as the taxi pulls up. Janice jumps out and the taxi goes to pull away.

MARTHA (*Still crying.*) Hang on, wait!
JANICE Oh, Mum, don't go.
MARTHA Just go into the house, Janice.

Martha gets into the taxi.

MARTHA Could you go back to where you've just come from, please?

The taxi driver looks confused but drives off.

SCENE 28. INTERIOR. BILL'S HOUSE: FRONT ROOM. NIGHT.
Winnie is looking out of the window, worried, when the taxi pulls up.

WINNIE (*Shouting.*) Here's our Martha, you've had it.

SCENE 29. EXTERIOR. BILL'S HOUSE: FRONT. NIGHT.
Winnie runs into the street and closes the front door behind her. We see Pauline rushing in the opposite direction with the six kids. Martha rushes up the path.

WINNIE He's locked me out. I can't get in, honest.

Martha goes around the side.

Look, he's not worth it, why worry yourself?

Martha doesn't listen.

He's just a maniac.

Martha opens the back yard and goes into the back. Winnie sits on the step and begins to cry.

SCENE 30. EXTERIOR. BILL'S HOUSE: BACK DOOR. NIGHT.
Martha presumes the door leading to the house is locked and so goes to the window.

MARTHA Let me in now, you bastard!
BILL (*Through window.*) Go on, piss off, ye' whore!
MARTHA Let me in now or I'm going to break this window. I'm not leaving until you're dead.
BILL (*Through window.*) Oh, yeah.

Smugly.

You'd try but I'd bleedin' murder you. So go on, piss off, you Miss high and mighty, get back to your restaurant and pretend you're better than everybody else. But we know what you really are, don't we, ay' ye' fat bastard?

Martha goes to the door leading to the kitchen and begins to bang it. She turns the handle and to her delight it is open.

MARTHA Right, you're gonna die!

SCENE 31. INTERIOR. BILL'S HOUSE: BACK ROOM. NIGHT.
Bill hears the door open. He jumps up and is obviously terrified.

BILL Get out! Get out, you're mad!
MARTHA (*Entering, puts her arms around his neck.*) I'm mad? I'm mad?
BILL Yeah. Go on, get out of my house.

Bill is choking.

You're choking me.
MARTHA Yeah, and I wish I'd done it twenty years ago.

She pushes him into the chair.

What's up with you? You crack up everytime one of us has a good time.

SCENE 32. EXTERIOR. BILL'S HOUSE: FRONT. NIGHT.
Winnie is sitting on the step still crying.

SCENE 33. INTERIOR. BILL'S HOUSE: BACK ROOM. NIGHT.

MARTHA When was the last time that my mum got a new dress or something? Well, that doesn't matter as long as you're in the pub twice a
day with everybody thinking you're bloody marvellous.

BILL (*Gets up.*) I'm sorry.

MARTHA A slag, why am I slag? Because I got divorced? You should be
on my side not Brian's. The only reason I got divorced was because
I didn't want to end up like my mum. So, now it's over and I'm
happy with somebody else. Somebody who buys me presents,
somebody who's not a bloody alcoholic. And so you say I'm a slag.
Well, if that's a slag that's what I want to be.

SCENE 34. EXTERIOR. BILL'S HOUSE: FRONT. NIGHT.
Winnie is sitting on the step when Brian and Marty come up the
path.

MARTY Is Martha here?

BRIAN Pauline sent us.

MARTY I don't know what's up with her, she's cracked up.

WINNIE I think she has, she's mad, there's been murder.

SCENE 35. INTERIOR. BILL'S HOUSE: BACK ROOM. NIGHT.

BILL I realise how bad I've been. I'll change.

MARTHA You'll never change. I just don't want me mum to be a nervous
wreck every time I'm on the phone.

BILL Martha, I promise. Come and visit me anytime.

MARTHA You're lucky I calmed down before. You could have been dead
now.

Martha leaves the room, Bill sits down with a massive sigh of relief.

SCENE 36. INTERIOR. BILL'S HOUSE: KITCHEN. NIGHT.
Winnie is standing at the stove. Brian and Marty hang about awk-
wardly and nervously as Martha enters.

MARTHA Iyah, Mart; sorry about that, Mum.

WINNIE I suppose he deserves it.

BRIAN (*Joking.*) Is he still alive?

MARTHA Unfortunately. But then again you probably caused all that by making me out to be a big slag in the pub.

BRIAN What are you talking about?

MARTHA As if you don't know. I'm going.

WINNIE Don't Martha, stay and have a cup of tea.

MARTHA No, I'll go.

BRIAN I'll walk down with you.

MARTHA Don't bother.

SCENE 37. EXTERIOR. STREET. NIGHT.
Brian and Martha walk together. It is pouring with rain.

BRIAN I gave Janice three pounds today.

MARTHA That was generous. How much did you spend in the pub?

BRIAN I wish things hadn't turned out like this.

MARTHA It's too late now.

BRIAN I wish it wasn't.

MARTHA Where are you going now?

BRIAN Me dad's.

MARTHA How nice.

BRIAN No, it's not.

MARTHA Don't be looking for pity.

They stop at the corner.

BRIAN Look, there's no reason why we still can't see each other every now and again.

MARTHA I'd rather not.

BRIAN Please yourself.

MARTHA I will. I never used to, but I'm pleasing myself now. I'm doing what I want to do. Without me mum, dad and you. I'm not going to let you pull me back. For the first time ever I'm quite happy.

BRIAN Are you really?

Martha doesn't answer.

MARTHA Well, I look like a drowned rat. I'm going.

BRIAN Are you going to little Kylie's christening next week?

MARTHA I think our Eileen must of cancelled it by now.

They both walk separate ways. Martha has tears in her eyes once again. Brian looks back. He too looks desperately sad. Martha turns to watch Brian going up the path of his dad's house. He sees her looking and waves. Embarrassed, she waves back. She turns around and continues walking into the distance.

The End.

Window of Vulnerability

(For Frans Montens 1947–1989)

Gregory Evans

SCENE 1. *INTERIOR. ESTHER'S FLAT: STAIRS. DAY.*
Esther sits on the stairs above a turn in the staircase. In the wall facing her, high above her head, a small window is open to the swelter of the summer's night. From time to time we hear, from outside, the ordinary night-time sounds of an inner city: distant shouting, car alarms, sirens. Esther's son, Joey, eight months old, sleeps on a towel at her feet.

ESTHER   The light from the stars cools me. It's the only thing that does. This is the coolest place in all the world. The starlight's cold. I know. It's come so far. Across all that empty dark. From stars that aren't there any more. Exploded. Died. Drifted into new constellations. This is old light.

The nights are so short now. Daylight's seeping into the sky already. No sleep again. I take the pills but they don't do much. Make me headachy. Slow me down. Make me long for sleep without giving it to me. They don't stop me thinking. No pills for that.

An item on the news last night. A couple starved their son to death. I think about that. A baby. Few months older than Joey. Nothing in his stomach but the rags of his nappy. I imagine his last hours. Caged in his cot. Too weak to cry.

SCENE 2. *STOCK FOOTAGE.*
Monochrome film of a razed and devastated city. It could be Hiroshima or Nagasaki; it could be Dresden.

Esther's voice continues.

ESTHER (*Voice over.*) Understanding nothing. Except that the world, the world he's seen so little of, it's a wretched bitter place. He must have been thankful to leave it. At the end he must have been glad. Another item. Same bulletin. A man was walking along a London street carrying a bag. A child's leg was sticking out. Not a hoax. People saw him. The police are treating it seriously. Looking along the banks of the Thames. Checking files of missing children. Why didn't someone go up to the man and stop him? Why didn't someone scream?

SCENE 3. INTERIOR. ESTHER'S FLAT: STAIRS. NIGHT.
As Scene 1.

ESTHER Joey can't sleep much either. He wailed when I put him down. His skin was hot and running with sweat and mine was the same, so I didn't know if I should take him in my arms, or leave him crying in his cot. In the end I brought him here. I gave him a suck and then I held him on my lap and we looked up together through the window. The moon was out, tiny and new, like one of Joey's nail-clippings.
The sky was deep blue, the blue before black, as if all the blues of the day were distilled into this one little square.
It calmed Joey, looking through the window, the way it always does. Sometimes I can't see me in his face at all. He looks so much like his father.

SCENE 4. INTERIOR. RUTH'S FLAT: KITCHEN. NIGHT.
A large, comfortable kitchen; there is an air of peace, of material comfort. French windows are open on to a garden. Pine; washing machine and dishwasher; a crowded noticeboard; pulses in jars. Framed posters decorate the walls: from exhibitions (The Tate, Whitechapel, maybe The Louvre or The Kroller-Müller), and older posters too, also framed, about Greenham and nuclear disarmament. There is a Greenpeace sticker on the window. A clock on the wall says three-thirty. In the middle of the kitchen is a table cluttered with files, books and papers. A low light hangs above it. Ruth has been working, probably still is: there is a chair pushed back, a glass of apple juice, a notepad, a dictaphone.
Ruth wears silk pyjamas: they are damp with sweat, clinging to her body. She stands at the sink, looking out of the window above it.

RUTH Jesus!

She turns on the cold tap, dips her head under the running water for a few seconds, comes up dripping. She rubs her hands over her scalp and the back of her neck. Then she towels herself dry.

I wonder, could this be the greenhouse effect we've been hearing so much about?

She unsticks her pyjamas from her skin.

Seems to me, it's a vicious circle. The hotter it gets, the more we need spray-on deodorants. The more we use those – the more the ozone layer breaks up. So it goes on getting hotter.

She crosses to the table, sits, looks momentarily blank.

Is this really a good idea, working at . . .

Looks at the clock, groans.

It's too hot to sleep. I'll feel like death tomorrow whatever I do. So why not? Clear some of the backlog.

She glances at the files.

I'd need to give up sleep altogether to clear it completely. Not impossible. I seem to have given up everything else. Smoking. Drinking. Sex, apparently. Is that machine switched on?

She checks the dictaphone. Then flicks through her notepad.

What was I doing?

She switches the dictaphone to 'play'.

DICTAPHONE (*Ruth's voice.*) . . . home-help reports that Mr Linden is incontinent.

RUTH (*Overlapping.*) Oh yes.

DICTAPHONE (*Ruth's voice continuing.*) He also hardly seems to be eating. Health visitor reports Mr Linden to be deteriorating rapidly. As there are apparently no living relatives and Mr Linden is unable to cope alone, it is imperative that we act asap. There is a problem.

RUTH (*Overlapping.*) There's always a bloody problem.

DICTAPHONE (*Ruth's voice.*) Jesus, this is stupid. I ought to go to bed, take a cold shower –

*She wipes the last couple of sentences; switches the dictaphone to
'record'.*

RUTH (*Into dictaphone.*) The problem is that Mr Linden refuses to go
into a home. He is willing to accept a place in sheltered accommo-
dation. By the time a sheltered flat becomes available, Mr Linden
will very probably be dead. I therefore have to call on Mr Linden
and persuade him of the joys and pleasures of living and dying . . .

She runs back the tape to wipe the last word.

. . . of living in an old people's home. I'd better go and see him first
thing tomorrow.

Ruth writes on her notepad.

I mean today.

Pause.

Next case.

She flicks over a few pages.

New referral. Esther Reeves. Details recorded by duty officer. Pre-
liminary notes in preparation for home visit. Which I'm due to
make . . . in about eight hours' time. Esther Reeves referred to us by
her GP . . . who is . . .

She picks up a letter.

. . . Dr Akhtar of the Unity Road Health Centre. Referral dated . . .
shit and derision! April! Four months! Dr Akhtar reports concern
about Esther Reeves' state of mind, her ability to cope alone with
her baby . . . also her financial difficulties, domestic arrangements,
her isolation, her diet . . .

Glances through the letter.

And just about everything else. Wonderful! Background from
health visitor. Esther Reeves has been a patient at Unity since falling pregnant eighteen months ago.

Pause.

Falling. Falling pregnant. Falling ill. Falling apart. Falling.

She shakes herself out of it; wipes that; sets the machine to 'record'.

Difficult pregnancy. Father absent. Difficult birth. Emergency Caesarean following protracted labour. And then things started to go downhill.

SCENE 5. INTERIOR. ESTHER'S FLAT: STAIRS. NIGHT.
As Scene 1. Esther is holding Joey in her arms now, singing to him.

ESTHER (*Sings.*) Hush little baby, don't you cry,
You know your mama was born to die.
All my trials, Lord, soon be over.
(*Normal speech.*) Your father was beautiful, Joey. Almost as beautiful as you. And he knew it! I think about him a lot. I think about him in this flat last summer. He was here for a week, a whole week. It was hot then too. Not hot like this, but hot enough. He used to lie in bed all day. Naked. The covers thrown back. I wrote him a letter after you were born. I sent it to the base. I don't know if he got it. I often wonder where he is. I don't even know whether he's still over here. He could have finished his tour by now. They might have sent him home. He could be somewhere even hotter than here. Nevada perhaps. Arizona. I said you were a boy. He'd have been pleased about that. He didn't want a girl. I mean, he didn't want a kid. He said he never wanted children. But a girl – certainly not a girl! He'd like to think he had a son though. I'm sure of it. He once told me that the bomb they dropped on Hiroshima was called 'Little Boy'.

Looks down at Joey.

Little boy. Strange. That pleased him, that sort of stuff. He thought it was *right*. The way things should be. He was always talking about it. Those weapons. What we've got, what the Russians have got. What it can all do.

Long Pause.

I don't know why they call it unthinkable. I think about it all the time. I try and push it to the back of my mind. It never stays there.

She looks up at the window.

We could escape through here, Joey. Get away from everything. Mothers murdering their children, fathers fucking them. All those bombs and missiles waiting for us. Through the other windows you'd just get to the city. This way you'd get to the stars.

She starts singing to Joey:

Hush little baby, don't you cry . . .

SCENE 6. STOCK FOOTAGE.

Images of the victims of Hiroshima and Nagasaki. Still photographs or newsreel footage.

Esther's voice continues.

ESTHER (*Voice over.*) You know your mama was born to die.
All my trials, Lord, soon be over.
I had a little book with pages three,
And every page spelled liberty.
All my trials, Lord, soon be over.
Too late, my brothers,
Too late, but never mind.
All my trials, Lord, soon be over.

SCENE 7. INTERIOR. ESTHER'S FLAT: KITCHEN. DAY.
(IN SOME CONTRAST TO RUTH'S KITCHEN.)

The window is open, looking out to other houses. Distant reggae. Esther sits at the kitchen table. By her feet, a bag of shopping spills its contents on to the floor. She has a glass of water and a bottle of tablets in front of her.

ESTHER A terrible thing happened.

She takes a tablet.

I wasn't going to use these today. I've got a woman coming soon. Social worker. Dr Akhtar said she could help us. I wanted to keep a clear head.

She takes another tablet, screws the cap on the bottle.

Look at me. Can't stop trembling even now.
I went out to the shop and left Joey asleep. I never do that. Hardly ever. He'd just gone down. He was lying there with his eyes half open. He often sleeps like that.

I closed them with the tips of my fingers and kissed the lids. He looked so peaceful. And he'd had such a bad night. I couldn't wake him. I had to get some nappies, we were right out. I wanted coffee too, so I could offer a cup to the woman when she comes. I had a last look at Joey. Then I ran. Almost flew down the stairs and out the front door. I cut through the playground by the community centre. It was littered with smashed bottles like it always is. And those little red-sealed plastic bags from the dope deals. Eddie used to slip out to the dealers. He said it was the only good thing about the place. Convenient hash.

I'd come through on to the street when I heard a screech of brakes just behind. I kept running. Then a voice. 'Stop!' Police.

Where had I come from? Where was I going? Why was I running? What was I carrying? Who did I speak to as I came through the playground?

One of the policemen told me to get in the van. I thought, they're going to take me away. I couldn't get my breath. I started shaking. All I could think of was Joey. He'd woken up. He was lying in his cot, crying for me. I could hear him. That's impossible, I know it now. But then I believed it. What could I do? I couldn't tell the police I'd left my baby alone. They searched me. There was a policewoman there so they had the right. Joey was screaming, I was sure of it. I suddenly thought about this social worker. I'd gone out, I'd left Joey alone – just when she was due to come round! How stupid can you get! If she knew that, or if she just didn't like what she saw – she could take him away from me.

Finally the police let me go. All I wanted was to run back here and pick Joey up and hold him. I managed to stop myself. I knew I had to walk on to the mini-market, walk on slowly as if nothing was wrong. I'd told them that's where I was going. So if I rushed straight home they might have got suspicious and followed me. I went round the shop in a daze. I didn't know what I was buying. I just dropped stuff in the basket.

I could hear Joey all the time. I got the coffee and the nappies though. Luck. When I got back here I threw up in the sink. Joey was still asleep. His eyes were half open again. Otherwise he hadn't moved.

The door bell rings.

That must be her. She's early.

The door bell rings again. Esther gets up.

SCENE 8. INTERIOR. RUTH'S FLAT: KITCHEN. EVENING.

Ruth sits at the table. She is working. The remains of a meal are pushed aside. In front of her: notebook, pen, dictaphone; and the inevitable glass of apple juice.

Ruth speaks into the dictaphone.

RUTH Case notes on Esther Reeves, following home visit made this a.m., six, seven, eighty-nine. I agree with Dr Akhtar (see letter of referral) that there is cause for concern about Esther Reeves. Her mental state, material circumstances. With possible implications for her capacity to care adequately for her child. Contrary to the opinion of the health visitor, I would say that at this stage it would be over-reacting . . .

She wipes the last word.

. . . it would be 'premature' to put the child's name on the at-risk register.

To herself as she flicks through her notebook.

General observations – her flat, her manner, response to my arrival . . .

Pause, then into dictaphone.

First of all, I'll deal with her state of mind, so far as I could ascertain it. Esther Reeves is . . .

She hesitates, sips her apple juice.

She's obviously suffering from anxiety. Exaggerated and irrational fears. Periodic depressions. Dr Akhtar points out that while her symptoms are not wholly compatible with post-natal depression, this is still a rather grey area.

Laughs.

Clinically speaking, I mean. So we shouldn't rule that out.

Longer pause.

Jesus!

Ruth rises. From the back of a cupboard she pulls out a bottle of vodka. Then she takes a glass from the draining-board and pours herself a drink. She goes back to her chair.

Esther Reeves is alone, bringing up a child. She is deeply troubled. She is desperately unhappy. And very, *very* afraid. Anxiety – yes. But then she's got cause to be anxious. She's certainly not inadequate. Or irrational. She's highly intelligent. And quite possibly the sanest person I've ever met. She is afraid for the future. No. Let me correct that. She cannot conceive of the future. Neither can I.

Pause.

Her fears centre around the threat of nuclear war. Nuclear holocaust.

Pause.
She takes a drink of vodka.

Threat.

Laughs.

Even now, now they're shaking hands and talking, sharing 'photo opportunities', even scrapping a few missiles here and there. It's not a threat. It's an overwhelming probability.

She takes another drink.

I used to think about it too, once: 'Nuclear Holocaust'. I used to think about it a lot. It became a preoccupation. An 'obsession'. I read books, went to meetings, I was conscientious – of course. I always am. I followed it all. Negotiations, arms talks. Deployment. I marched and demonstrated. Camped at Greenham Common. I learned all the arguments, the facts and figures. Megatons. Warheads. Kill probabilities.

Pause.

The explosive yield of the world's nuclear arsenal is the equivalent of twenty billion tons of TNT. That's to say, one million six hundred thousand Hiroshimas. By now probably more. You can even work it out as so much for each of us, so many tons of nuclear death for every man, woman and child on earth. What does that mean? I've forgotten what it means. It's stopped meaning anything. She knows. Oh, not the statistics, like I do. But she understands.

Longer pause.

I'd been there for some time. It was coming to the end of the visit. I just wanted to go, to get away. She gave me her baby son to hold. She was making another cup of coffee; which I didn't want. Joseph, the little boy. Joey, she calls him. He didn't mind being passed to a stranger at all. He didn't cry. I held him on my lap, while she moved about the kitchen, talking. I'd stopped trying to be professional by then – though I don't know if she noticed.

Pause.

'If it happens', she said, 'if it happens, and if we survive, I should have to kill him.'

Pause.

'I should have to kill my son', she said. 'And then I should have to kill myself. I think about that. I worry about that a lot.'
It took me a moment to understand. At first I didn't know what she meant. I almost said: If what happens?

She takes another drink.

The problem, as she sees it . . . the problem is . . . that we're chronically brutal and vicious. By 'we' she means the human race. Mankind. To put it simply: she does not believe that we're good enough to survive.

Longer pause.

When I first arrived, her son was asleep in the next room. He woke up, and she went to fetch him. She held him on her lap. He was crying a bit, still dopey from sleep. We hadn't got on to . . . to the matter discussed above. I was still talking about benefits and helplines, getting out of the flat more, and meeting some other mums. As she was listening to me, she kissed her son – Joey – on the top of his head. Quite casually. I watched her face. Such love. Such love.

Ruth is close to tears.

These thoughts. They're not good. This is all no good. It does nothing for anybody.

She runs the tape back, sets it to 'play'.

DICTAPHONE (*Ruth's voice.*) . . . highly intelligent. And quite possibly the sanest –

Ruth winds the tape back a little more, again sets it to 'play'.

DICTAPHONE (*Ruth's voice.*) . . . I'll deal with her state of mind, so far as I could ascertain it –

She stops the tape. Sets it to 'record'.

RUTH I concur with Dr Akhtar's diagnosis that, despite certain symptomatic discrepancies, Esther Reeves is most probably suffering from post-natal depression. Which is clearly exacerbated by her material circumstances.

Pause.

There are specific strategies for treating this.

SCENE 9. INTERIOR. ESTHER'S FLAT: BEDROOM. NIGHT.
Overhead shot: Esther lies in bed, with the covers thrown back. Joey lies beside her, in the crook of her arm. Both are asleep.

SCENE 10. STOCK FOOTAGE.

The weapons, waiting. Soviet SS20s in snowy forests. American Cruise missiles in the English countryside. Silos in the Nevada Desert. Nuclear submarines at Holy Loch. F1-11s taking off at dawn.

On the soundtrack we hear Esther singing the lullaby to Joey.

ESTHER (*Voice over.*) Hush little baby, don't you cry,
You know your mama was born to die.
All my trials, Lord, soon be over.
I had a little book with pages three,
And every page spelled liberty.
All my trials, Lord, soon be over.
There grows a tree in Paradise
And pilgrims call it the tree of life.
All my trials, Lord, soon be over.

Scene 11. Interior. Esther's Flat: Bedroom. Night.
Esther and Joey asleep, as in Scene 9.

ESTHER (*Voice over.*) If living were a thing that money could buy,
the rich would live and the poor would die.
Too late, my brothers,
Too late, but never mind.
All my trials, Lord, soon be over.

Repeat chorus if necessary.

The End.

The Conversion of St Paul

Robert Flynn

Music by Kevin Murray

SCENE 1. EXTERIOR. CORNER PUB. NIGHT.

A town in north-eastern Scotland. On the corner of the intersection of two streets formed by high stone buildings, a pub with large, frosted windows begins to glow in the twilight. To the south is a river silvered by the moon and spanned by two long bridges; a concrete road bridge and an old, dark curving railway bridge. The pub is on the edge of a dockland area in an old part of a town which has been gutted of its history by demolition and haphazard re-building. From the top of the street, the river is hidden by the road bridge approach flyover which leads, in a long concrete curve, to the road bridge toll booths. Cars swish past and up to the bridge, lights beginning to flare in the half-light, as they head for the toll booths which are illuminated from above by large lamps. A large land-scaped area has been formed below the huge concrete slabs that support the bridge approaches, paths leading through shrubs, young trees and grass to the parapet that follows the river out to the sea. A large slab of a new, prison-like hotel lies to the west along with a towering office block. The hotel's casino lights begin to glow blue, glimpsed over the small, land-locked lighthouse that sits incongruously in the landscaped gardens below the approach road. The streets around the pub are empty, Twilight hovers in the cool air, sharply outlining the stone building.

Music: Broken jazz introduction.

An old Volvo Estate pulls up to the entrance to the pub. A thin, haggard girl, Trisha, hitches up her coat and short skirt and gets out of the passenger seat, dips her head back into the car then stands back, closes the door and, as the car pulls away, stuffs some money in her handbag and takes out a cigarette, lights it with slightly unsteady hands, considers the awning above the pub with the illuminated sign 'Glengarry Lounge' then walks up to the entrance, opens the door and disappears inside. Her high heels clack on the pavement, crossing a circular, old-fashioned mosaic which is set into the pavement slabs in front of the pub entrance – a picture of a Glengarry bonnet with The Glengarry Lounge arranged around it.

Music: Muffled jazz inside.

We close in on a window of the pub. The window streams with condensation caused by the heat inside, shadows, vague shapes of the people inside, move on the window. The watery shape of a hand moves up to the window from inside and, in the mist of the condensation, writes 'St Paul'.

Music: Muffled playing of a fast bebop version of Scrapple from the Apple *(Charlie Parker).*

SCENE 2. INTERIOR. CORNER PUB. NIGHT.
Pull back from window on which 'St Paul' is written.

Behind the blaring bell of a trumpet, a young man, his face screwed up with concentration, sweat on his brow, plays the last notes of his improvisation on the jazz standard played by a small band on a small stage area formed in the middle of the pub. The band, in contrast, are four middle-aged men in casual clothes and play sloppily in comparison to the fast, bright, finishing run of the trumpeter, Paul.

Paul is slim, pale, intense, in the hot, smoky atmosphere he is dressed in a white shirt with glaring fifties tie, black braces support his black trousers. Listening to the band are a mixed crowd of middle-aged and young people, some crowded at the bar facing the stage, some at scattered tables and chairs. The pub is dingy, hot, slightly run-down but doing good business; groups of hard-looking women are chatted up by men in jeans and jackets and white socks and polished black shoes. A young girl, who has just written 'St Paul' on the window, turns in her seat and stares away from the glass at the trumpeter as the band go into the last moments of the number.

Music: Jazz band now playing very loudly.

Trisha slides her way past the knots of people, signals to the gum-chewing barmaid and is quickly handed a whisky. She takes a long sip, working it around her mouth and holding it in her throat before swallowing it. As she takes the almost empty glass from her lips, she looks nervously at a big man who leans on the bar handing out drinks for a group of laughing men in overcoats and askew ties, the big man is telling an unheard story to the men. He is in command, his voice lost below the jazz music. He has the blue complexion of a heavy drinker, his belly hanging out over his slacks, poking out from his blazer. His eyes slide in his debauched face towards Trisha and he winks. She smiles a false, faltering movement of her lips which are over-painted with red.

The Blue Man signals to the barmaid to serve the girl another drink and then goes back to his story, nodding his head sideways towards her. The men he is with burst into hard laughter, glancing her way. A glass, full of whisky, is put in front of her.

An old Wino in tattered coat and ragged shoes watches Paul play, his dulled eyes lightened by the music, a grin on his stubbled face. He carries a plastic bag. He fumbles in his pockets and turns away from the band, nodding his head in time to the music, struggles out some silver and shuffles to the bar, ready to buy a drink. The Blue Man stands in front of him. The Wino is oblivious to the Blue Man who reaches out his big hand and squeezes the Wino's face in a vicious grip that sinks into the cheeks of the startled face of the down-and-out. The Blue Man starts to walk forward, forcing the Wino backwards through the crowd which parts in silence.

Paul, playing the last few bars of the number, flicks scared eyes over to the action as the Wino is forced out. From behind his fingers working on his gleaming trumpet, his eyes lock on Trisha's. He sees his terror reflected in hers as the Blue Man grins and forces the Wino through the door.

SCENE 3. EXTERIOR. CORNER PUB. NIGHT.
The Wino falls heavily, backwards, on to the pavement, covering the Glengarry mosaic, pushed by the Blue Man. His face is marked with red lines from the hands of the Blue Man and tears well up in

his eyes. Some of his coins go spinning and rolling into the drain in the gutter by his head. The Blue Man looks on, grinning, impassive, then walks back into the pub. Wiping the tears and snot from his nose, the Wino starts to stagger to his feet.

Scene 4. Interior. Corner pub. Night.

Music: Coda.

Paul blasts out the last, high notes of the number and the band finish, late, behind him. The Blue Man strides back in, through the crowd, strutting, arrogant. He nods to various people as they clap the band on stage. Paul shakes the spittle from his trumpet, watching as the Blue Man rests his hand on Trisha's hip, speaking into her ear as she finishes her whisky. The heavy-set Drummer of the band, wearing a sweat shirt and jeans, goes to the microphone at the centre of the stage.

DRUMMER Thanks, ladies and gentlemen, we're taking a short break now but the Savoys will be back in a wee while.

Music: Pet Shop Boys comes on from the wall speakers as the Drummer speaks.

Paul takes the mouthpiece off his trumpet and fits the instrument into a small, immaculate case. The rest of the band huddle together on the stage, excluding Paul as pints of heavy and lager are handed over to them by a barmaid. Paul shrugs on a black jacket and bends to snap the instrument case shut. He concentrates on his case and looks up, surprised, as the Girl who had written 'St Paul' on the window presents herself in front of him. The babble of conversation goes on in the pub. Raucous laughter and leers from the girls in the corner. Paul begins to step off stage.

GIRL *(Flutters her eyes.)* Hiya, gorgeous, fancy using your lips for something else?

Music.

Paul doesn't reply, gets up and hurries through the crowd towards the door of the pub, the Girl stares after him, shaking her head, helpless, laughing.

*Paul walks past the musicians standing, smoking and drinking at
the side of the stage. He carries his instrument case. He nods shyly to
them as he passes. The Drummer shouts to him as he passes.*

DRUMMER Paul

*Paul turns to him, smiling, then the drummer waves his hand
dismissively at him.*

. . . ah, never mind, away and play your lonesome jubilee, son, just
be back in time.

*The Blue Man walks up to the musicians as Paul leaves through the
entrance doors of the pub. He has his arm around Trisha, who looks
tired, jumpy, she is excluded from any conversation. The Blue Man
talks to the Drummer. Nods towards the departing figure of Paul.*

BLUE MAN When's that laddie gonna see sense and leave before you
drag him doon ta your level?

DRUMMER What? Paul? Takes more'n a good lip to go places. Listen, six
weeks he's been playing with us, for nothin'. Says he just wants to
play, can you believe that?

BLUE MAN (*Half joking.*) Christ, he's better than you lot, any way.

DRUMMER (*Laughs along with Blue Man.*) He's a'right, he'll never make
it. Wet behind the ears. Nae confidence. Listen, he dosnae even
take a drink, just goes away for a wander then comes back for the
set, like a fuckin' ghost.

Laughs.

BLUE MAN Maybe he's a poof, better watch yer backs, boys.

The musicians laugh, too loudly.

Be back shortly. Look after the premises for me, and nae drinkin'
anymore a ma beer, you get enough outta me.

Voice turns nasty, irrational.

An' turn it doon next time, right?

SCENE 5. EXTERIOR. APPROACH FLYOVER ROAD. NIGHT.
Paul ducks under the first curve of the approach flyover road situated about 100 yards from the pub, leading to the bridge that crosses the river, the banks of which are just beyond the landscaped area ahead of Paul.

SCENE 6. EXTERIOR. BRIDGE APPROACHES. NIGHT.
Paul walks along a secluded path underneath the towering approaches. Lights reflect off cars in the deserted car parking area below the concrete. Huge pillars support the road and they cast large, sudden areas of shadow over the sparse trees and foliage below. Paul walks from light to shadow, shadow to light, past the pillars towards the gleaming river that is about 50 yards in front of him.

SCENE 7. EXTERIOR. APPROACH FLYOVER ROAD. NIGHT.
The Blue Man hauls a reluctant Trisha under the curve of the approach road, near to where Paul has just gone.

SCENE 8. EXTERIOR. PARAPET AND LOW RAILINGS BY THE RIVER. NIGHT.
Paul leans against the railing by the parapet on the river bank.

Music: River theme.

He lights a cigarette, pulls in a gulp of smoke and visibly relaxes, leans forward, elbows on the railings, staring over the water, lost in thoughts and concerned dreams. The night is silent, deserted. To his left, cars light up the night as they speed across the bridge, to his right, further up the river, the iron girders of the old rail bridge criss-cross into the distance. A train hoots across the water as it crosses. A large moon hangs above the rippling river. Paul is relaxed, comforted by the night and the river view and dreams of escape. His trumpet case rests at his feet. He leans back and blows a cloud of blue smoke into the air. Voices play in his head, voices that become a kind of music.

Music: River theme fades to. . . .

Scene 9. Exterior. Parapet and low railings by river. Night.
Music: Traffic mixed with moans and musical textures.

Paul looks at his watch, finishes his smoke, throws the butt into the river, picks up his case and starts to walk back the way he came. As he walks by the river's edge, he watches the winking light of a small aircraft as it sails into the sky.

Scene 10. Exterior. Bridge approaches. Night.
Paul walks back along the pathway, appearing in and out of the shadows thrown by the pillars supporting the bridge approaches. A small moan issues from the end of the pillars, only just heard in the still night air.

Paul, walking quickly, starts to slow, a look of worry and caution on his face as he hears moans and grunts and gasps that get louder as he nears the end of the approach road flyover.

Paul slows down, fear on his face, as he nears the last pillar, the noise of a soft fight, an animal noise of quick, forced sex, the wet groans and grunts of a man and the high sound of a woman, assail his ears. The noises come from an area directly in front of him, where the last pillar blocks his view, beyond which is a walled-in section.

Paul walks silently to the last pillar, behind which something is causing guttural noises, something happening in the shadows between the pillar and the wall. He turns and leans his head against the last pillar. His face is taut, eyes flickering, he is breathing quickly, softly, he is sweating slightly. He hears the shuffle of clothes, the final gasp of the man. Then he hears a slap, followed by the dull thud of a punch and the pained cry of a woman. The man's voice comes muffled, barking. Paul's breath comes in gasps. He squeezes his eyes tight and grimaces as he hears a scream from behind the pillar. He is frightened, disgusted, he looks at his watch, his head turns in consternation, indecision. He drops his case and turns around the damp concrete pillar.

SCENE 11. *EXTERIOR. APPROACH FLYOVER ROAD. NIGHT.*
Paul stands surveying the scene, the act that has taken place in
the shadows between the concrete pillar and wall of the flyover.
The Blue Man stands over Trisha who is sprawled on the ground,
beside the banking where some shrubs have been planted. She is
half-clothed, holding her stomach, she still wears her coat but her
skirt is torn. The Blue Man is in a violent, red-faced rage, shouting
at her.

BLUE MAN Come on then, come, d'ye want some more. Stop yer greetin', ye've had worse than that.

Paul, completely composed, walks slowly up to Trisha, who looks at
him in astonishment. The Blue Man gapes at him in total surprise,
taken aback, he does nothing to stop Paul who walks between him
and the girl.

BLUE MAN What's this, it's the jazz man.

Becomes more confident, taunting.

Hey, poof, piss off, its nane a' your business, get back to yer horn

Becomes annoyed.

d'you hear me?

The Blue Man watches in a kind of amused astonishment as Paul
ignores him and reaches down to pick up Trisha, straightens her
clothes and hugs her. She weeps against his chest, in big, breathless
bursts.

BLUE MAN (*Arrogance turning to wild-eyed rage.*) Ah, well, that's nice. The whore and the poof. Watch it, prick, or she'll do a number on you.

Shouting in sudden rage.

Leave her, she's mine, she *belongs* to me. D'you know who I am? I'll have you *hurt* for this. I'm gonna stuff that trumpet up your arse, boy.

The Blue Man moves forward, kicks the instrument case away, fist
clenches. He takes a thin knife out of his pocket and moves towards
Paul who slowly, calmly, releases his grip of Trisha, turns to face

him. Trisha shakes her head, clutches at Paul's arm, trying to pull him away. The Blue Man moves in.

Paul opens his mouth wide, and cries out a mingled roar and a scream of frightening intensity, a shout of pure anger, a sonic blast of released frustration and unleashed hate and sorrow. The sound echoes in the enclosed concrete space.

The Blue Man is knocked back against the concrete wall by the shout of Paul. His knees buckle and he sprawls back, his legs twisted under him, his body partially supported by the wall. His head cracks against the wall, his eyes close, his mouth slackens. Paul stands trembling, the shout still echoing around the space, Trisha cowers behind him, staring at the crushed heap of the Blue Man. Coins spill from his pocket as he falls.

Trisha rushes over to the Blue Man's body, reaches in his pockets and brings out wads of notes, she hurries back to where Paul stands, as if in a trance, picks up her handbag, stuffs some of the notes inside. She puts her arm around his shoulders, draws him down to her and gently kisses his forehead and then his lips, then hands him the wad of money. He shakes his head. She opens his jacket and forces it into his pocket. She walks unsteadily over to where his instrument case has been kicked, lifts it, and presents it to him. She looks at Paul, unsure, awed, disturbed.

SCENE 12. EXTERIOR. LANDSCAPED AREA BY BRIDGE. NIGHT. Paul and Trisha walk along the path leading from the flyover where flowers and trees ruffle in the breeze. They pass a land-locked lighthouse resting in the middle of a flower bed. Trisha pulls at Paul's free arm and links her arm in with his. They walk slowly towards the pub, like a couple who have just discovered they love each other.

The Wino nervously gulps some cheap wine from the bottle and watches as Paul and Trisha stroll past, he is crouching in the bushes behind the lighthouse. As he watches them his face turns from nervous glaring to repose and calm. He moves out of frame leaving the bottle swaying on the earth. Suddenly his hand comes back into frame to grab the bottle away.

SCENE 13. EXTERIOR. APPROACH FLYOVER ROAD. NIGHT.
The Wino staggers out from the foliage into the area where the Blue Man lies in a heap. The Wino, bottle in hand, weaves warily around the flattened figure, looks around, confused and suspicious, then moves towards the coins that have scattered on the ground where the Blue Man had fallen a few minutes before. Very gently, the Wino begins picking up the coins in his hands until they are falling from his grip, he is spilling a lot of the wine he is carrying in the process. He jumps back as the Blue Man groans, his head moving from side to side then falling back. The Wino puts the coins in his pockets but they fall through his ragged raincoat to the ground. He spits in frustration, looks around, then puts the wine bottle at the feet of the Blue Man. As he does, he spots the luxurious coat which the Blue Man had discarded earlier lying against the wall. The Wino looks down at his own tattered coat and back to the expensive coat on the ground and smiles.

SCENE 14. EXTERIOR. CORNER PUB. NIGHT.
Illuminated by the diffused light of the pub Paul and Trisha disengage arms. Trisha stops, holds him with her arms outstretched and stares at him as if to imprint him on her memory. She knows she will not see him again. She drops her arms, smiles. The muffled sound of the band starting up inside causes Paul to listen for a moment. He walks towards the main entrance to the pub leaving Trisha staring after him on the corner.

SCENE 15. INTERIOR. CORNER PUB. NIGHT.
Paul walks confidently through the figures in the pub, people part for him to pass. The Drummer glares at him as he mounts the stage, the band in the middle of a number, sounding shabby without him.

SCENE 16. EXTERIOR. CORNER PUB. NIGHT.
Trisha leans against the wall of the pub, one foot bent against the stone, like a young girl with an air of innocence about her, staring into the middle distance, happily lost.

SCENE 17. INTERIOR. CORNER PUB. NIGHT.
Paul coolly fits the mouthpiece to his trumpet watched side-on by the astonished band.

SCENE 18. EXTERIOR. CORNER PUB. NIGHT.
Trisha's reverie is broken as a large evil-looking car with tinted windows pulls up beside her and, with engine still purring, the back passenger door opens slowly towards her. She straightens up, adjusting her skirt.

SCENE 19. INTERIOR. CORNER PUB. NIGHT.
Music: Broken jazz lead-in to waltz.
Paul puts the trumpet to his lips and begins to play a series of fast phrases that are discordant, a wild counterpoint to the band's playing.

SCENE 20. EXTERIOR. CORNER PUB. NIGHT.
Trisha moves a step towards the car, smiling her false come-on smile, leans forward and holds the top of the car door. Suddenly, Paul's trumpet can be heard as clear as a bell from inside the pub. Her smile fades.

SCENE 21. INTERIOR. CORNER PUB. NIGHT.
Paul, his face screwed up in a kind of passion, plays on, overwhelming the band. People stop drinking and talking, watching him nervously, disturbed by this figure of strange power, everyone becoming still.

SCENE 22. EXTERIOR. CORNER PUB. NIGHT.
Trisha hesitates at the door of the car which awaits her then slams the door shut with a determined fury, folds her coat around her then steps away. The car immediately pulls away, rounds the corner and is gone. The music from the pub swells and builds into the night air and she throws back her head, intent on the sound.

SCENE 23. INTERIOR. CORNER PUB. NIGHT.
Paul plays on and as he does the lights fade around him, leaving the frozen figures of the band and the crowd in the dark as he is backlit, soaring into escape with the music that swirls around him.

SCENE 24. EXTERIOR. CORNER PUB. NIGHT.

The Wino faces Trisha, proudly wearing the Blue Man's overcoat. She laughs as he dramatically takes a large cigar case out of the pocket, pulls out a cigar, runs it below his nose, strikes a match against the sole of his still battered shoe and lights it, all in the best W. C. Fields melodramatic style. By this time Trisha is giggling, something she hardly felt before, true happiness. The Wino bows low from the waist and sweeps his hand towards the entrance to the pub.

Soundtrack music swells.

WINO It has been many a year since any lady felt ah wis fit tae accompany anythin' other than a dog, but ah would be honoured if the young lass would consider the next dance.

SCENE 25. INTERIOR. CORNER PUB. NIGHT.

Paul finishes in a welter of notes, eventually blowing the trumpet away from his lips, takes a deep triumphant breath, there is silence in the darkened pub.

Soundtrack music plays on.

He dismantles his trumpet, puts it in the case and walks out of the pool of light. Into the pool of light step Trisha and the Wino, holding each other's hands before beginning to waltz to the soundtrack music.

SCENE 26. EXTERIOR. APPROACH FLYOVER ROAD. NIGHT.

Two policemen pick up the groggy Blue Man. One sniffs the wine bottle at his feet, grimaces. The other shoves the Wino's discarded raincoat over the Blue Man's shoulders. They lead him away to their car in the background.

SCENE 27. EXTERIOR. PARAPET BY RIVER. NIGHT.

Paul grips the parapet, his eyes full of anticipation and excitement looking across to the other shore as if he wanted to throw himself over there. He turns and begins a fast jog towards the steps leading up to the road bridge pedestrian walkway.

SCENE 28. EXTERIOR. LANDSCAPED AREA BY BRIDGE. NIGHT.
*The police car that now contains the stunned Blue Man races off,
light revolving and flashing, passes the land-locked folly of the lighthouse in the gardens. As it does the lighthouse beams out a revolving
beam of light, illuminating the waterfront, throwing it into light
and dark and light. Paul's fleeting figure is caught for a moment.*

SCENE 29. INTERIOR. CORNER PUB. NIGHT.
*Trisha and the Wino twirl in a fast waltz, coats fanning out
behind them in the pool of light. They are both blissful.*

SCENE 30. EXTERIOR. ROAD BRIDGE PEDESTRIAN WALKWAY. NIGHT.
*Paul runs along the straight line of the pedestrian walkway situ-
ated in the middle of the road bridge as cars flash past on either side.
He swings his trumpet case as the lights beam down on his lone running figure. On either side the river is made into liquid silver by the
moon.*

*A train clacks over the railway bridge that runs parallel over the
river, as if following him. Paul runs on, along a straight road south
that seems to lead into infinity or the heavens.*

Fade.

The End.

Breast is Best

Paula Macgee

SCENE. INTERIOR. 'DINER DOLLS'. DAY.
Black space – in the centre of the picture, some distance away, we see a woman seated at a table nursing her baby. Above her is a red neon strip light, seemingly without support, stating 'Diner Dolls'. We are in a symbolic American diner – the table should be dressed as appropriate: garish and loud, a caricature of itself.

Robert Palmer's 'Addicted to Love' is playing.

Slow track in on woman, who gradually becomes distinguishable. As she does so, the music fades out and a cot chime lullaby fades up.

As we reach the woman the lullaby fades out. Mother looks up from baby and speaks directly to camera.

MOTHER I'll have a glass of milk please . . .

Recognises Server.

Hi! How are you? God, it's ages since I've seen you. I didn't recognise you with your hair all blonde like that. You were just about to go away last time I was in, weren't you, that's right, your flight date was the same day as he (*To baby.*) was due. Remember, I tried to convince you to swap places.

Laughs.

God, it's good to see you . . . It's great to be out . . .

To baby.

Our first venture out into the big bad world, eh wee one? What a hassle! It takes me about half an hour to get the pushchair unfolded, never mind anything else. Oh, by the way, I left it by the door. I pushed it right into the corner, so I don't think it's in anyone's way. Listen, I'd better not keep you. Why don't you come over at your break, we could have a chat. If I can remember how to do it.

Mother and baby are chilled by a gust of wind. We see her hair being blown from her face.

God, it's cold with the door open like that, no, no, we're fine . . . but look at you, you've got goosebumps all up and down your arms – have you not got a jumper or anything? No, I suppose not. Hardly match the outfit would it? How's your wee one. A wee girl, isn't it? Apple of your eye I'll bet.

Mother looks at baby.

We've called him Martin after his Daddy. He is big, isn't he? It's all this good food he's getting.

The Mother discreetly lifts up her T-shirt and feeds her son.

He'd have me sucked raw given half the chance.

CUSTOMER'S VOICE (*Voice over.*) Excuse me.

Server's glance moves swiftly round, taking in the blur of neon strip. Stops dead on Customer.
Close-up of disapproving, almost caricatured face of Customer.
Music out – two loud horn blasts. As in 'Addicted to Love'.
Swift pan through neon strip back to Mother.

MOTHER You'd better go.

As at beginning – slow track from a distance, on to Customer seated at diner table. Same music as before.

CUSTOMER (*To Server.*) So glad you could fit me in between chats – I'll have a 'Tropical Tantaliser' *with* cherries. Friend of yours, is she? Disgusting behaviour if you ask me. There's a time and a place for everything, that's what I always say and sitting in a public restaurant isn't one of them . . . Of course my Harold was in catering. Couldn't stomach that kind of thing, well what decent man would. When I was feeding my Josephine he'd make me up a lovely tray and leave it on the cistern. He'd always put a little cushion on the toilet seat, and leave me at it for an hour or so, while he went out and read the evening paper or whatever.

Cut to image of Harold sitting in parlour reading 'Playboy'.

I think he enjoyed the time to himself really. Such a considerate man. I was very lucky.

She scans the menu.

Oh, and I'll have a 'Samantha Fox' shake please, raspberry. Of course, it's these trendy lefties I blame, they're all for this feeding lark, but women like myself, of good breeding and background, want it done in the home behind closed doors – I mean look . . .

She strains in her seat to get a good look.

You can see everything.

She gags.

Oh . . . it's enough to put you off your food . . . if I had any, will I have to wait long, dear? Oh and before you go, would you clear this up please – I got such a fright when she pulled it out . . . I knocked over the wee carnation.

Camera gaze moves slowly away from Customer, to an open newspaper spread out on the table – it is open at 'Page 3'. A carnation in its Perrier bottle has spilt over the page. There is a very young-looking Page 3 model, with the headline 'Sexy Suzie, Sweet 16'.

Music – four horn blasts 'Addicted to Love' alternating from 'Suzie's Boobs' to close-up of Mother feeding baby. The final blast should end up on Mother, who looks up and addresses Server.

MOTHER (*She now has her milk. She is having some bother getting her son to latch on.*) I won't be a minute.

To baby.

C'mon, darling, settle down, that's it, that's a boy, good, that's good, isn't it?

She takes a long drink of milk.

God, I needed that. It's incredible, I'm thirsty all the time. A bit like him really. Do you know I'm drinking four pints of milk a day, it's unbelievable. I feel like I'm turning into a huge fat cow.

Laughing.

I suppose I am really, look at me. Whatever happened to slimcea me of yesterday? I feel like I've had silicon implants. Demand feeding, very demanding. Every hour, on the hour. He's like a little limpet (*Looks at baby.*), a wonderful, wonderful little limpet.

She moves in her seat and winces as she does so.

Oh, God (*Sardonically.*) You wouldn't happen to have a rubber ring, would you? They make sitting so much easier. Wonderful things, rubber rings. They'll never remind me of Butlins again. I should have brought it with me, but it's a bit embarrassing carrying 'Donald Duck's Splashtime Fun Ring' everywhere I go. I suppose I should be thankful for small mercies. At least I *can* sit down. A major achievement, believe you me. God, it's so good to be out, so good to be out with him.

She looks down at baby who is still feeding. Server's gaze focuses in on the baby at the breast.

Music – horns from 'Addicted to Love', four blasts. With each blast we focus sharply on the picture of 'Sexy Suzie', finally focusing on the breasts. The image then begins to spin rapidly and the breasts transform into the 'Tropical Tantaliser'. Two mounds of ice cream, placed in a split banana.

MANAGER'S VOICE With cherries, just as Madam ordered.

Two cherries magically appear on the ice cream.

Server's gaze then takes in Customer and Manager as though looking at them from the Mother's table.

CUSTOMER (*To Manager standing beside table.*) I'm sorry, but that's the way it is, I couldn't possibly enjoy my 'Tropical Tantaliser' with *that* going on over there – so if you're not going to do anything about it, you can bring me my coat – I'm sure you'll find someone else to eat the sweet.

Server's gaze moves swiftly over neon strip and stops at Mother. She now has her coffee.

MOTHER (*Still feeding.*) Could I have another glass of milk, please? I'll need to give him the other side before I burst.

She looks at her blouse.

Oh no, this was clean on today.

She rubs a damp patch at her breast.

(*To Server.*) Can you hold him for a minute?

She holds the baby out to camera.

MANAGER'S VOICE (*Out of vision.* Sickly sweet.) Excuse me.

Server's glance moves swiftly round over neon sign, stops dead on close-up of Manager's face, as seen through a fish-eye lens. He looks suitably seedy.

Two horn blasts.

Back to Mother once again over strip light.

MOTHER You'd better go.

As at beginning, slow track with same music in to Manager. Above his head is a strip light saying 'Toilet'. As we draw nearer, the Manager's face changes from 'sickly sweet' to aggressive. The Server's gaze will move to the left as though trying to escape.

MANAGER C'm here you.

Server's gaze corrects itself, and ends up face to face with the Manager who is holding a 'Sam Fox' shake, umbrella and all.

What are you tryin' to do to me? Ruin my business? As soon as word gets out that we encourage that kind of behaviour, you can kiss 'bye bye' to your three-course business lunch for £1.95 bri-gade. And you know I've got the photographer from the *Echo* com-ing this afternoon. Now I'm not a hard man. I've put a chair in the toilet, I've even moved the disposal bin, to give her a bit more room. The toilet needed a bit of a clean, but I put the lid down, so she'll never know the difference.

We hear the sound of a toilet flushing, we slow fade on to a rather grubby-looking toilet with a disposal bin, on the lid of which is a sticker saying 'Now wash your hands please'.

As we focus on the sticker the flushing gets louder. The Manager's head invades the Server's gaze on the sticker, and pushes it back. Broadening out the shot.

So I'm telling you, if Mumsie wants to do the business, she can do it in the bog. I want that woman over there to eat, enjoy and pay for her 'Tropical Tantaliser' and she isn't going to do that, is she, as long as your friend over there keeps pushing them out for all the world to see. It's not that I object, but that's not the point is it? It's the principle of the thing. So you can get over there and tell her it's either in the bog, or out the door. Oh and before you do, make sure she pays for her milk.

Manager turns to walk away. Turns back when Server doesn't move.

Well, what are you waiting for? Can't bring yourself to do it, can we? Bit beneath you, is it? Well, just you listen to me, you work for me, I pay your wages and unless you do what I tell you, you can join Mummy dear over there on the bloody pavement! Got it? Good.

There is the sound of a glass smashing. The Server's gaze falls to the floor where the Manager has dropped the 'Sam Fox' shake.

An' you can clear that up as well.

Server's gaze then follows a thick oozy stream of milk shake as it winds its way across the black floor, under the table and through the legs of the complaining Customer, until it eventually ends up at the Mother's table. Server looks at Mother.

MOTHER (*Still feeding.*) It's a wonder I get time to do anything else. I
thought I might have a Kingsize Burger, no relish please, but
there's no rush. You can finish cleaning up if you want, I'll need to
wait until 'gannet features' has had enough anyway. Maybe I could
move to another table, make it easier for you to get under. No, No,
it's no trouble. There's actually a bit of a draught here, I'd probably
be better moving, if that's OK with you.

She starts moving.

MANAGER'S VOICE Hello there!

*Server sees smiling 'fish-eyed' face of Manager, whose gold filling
glints ('ring-of-confidence' style). Server's gaze even takes in both
Manager and Mother. Manager never meets the Mother's gaze for
fear of catching sight of (horror of horrors!) a nipple. He misinter-
prets her moving.*

So good of you to understand. Not everyone's cup of tea, that's the
thing.

MOTHER I beg your pardon?

MANAGER Puts some people off their food, you see. One of my custom-
ers actually felt a bit sicky-wicky. It's not that I've anything against
it personally, it's just that we just don't have the facilities here, a bit
like wheelchairs really.

MOTHER Sorry?

MANAGER No, no! No need to be sorry. Now just this once I've set up a
wee chair for you in the toilet. If you need anything, just bang on
the door. Someone's bound to hear you as they pass. Would you
like a magazine, I'm sure we've got a *Woman's Own* kicking about
here somewhere?

MOTHER In the toilet. You want me to feed in the toilet?

To Server.

You didn't tell me – you ought to have told me.

*As at beginning of scene, wind blows and dishevels Manager and
Mother.*

MANAGER (*Looking towards the door.*) Shit, it's him.

Sickly sweet.

Hello!

MOTHER (*To Server.*) Would you eat your dinner in a toilet?

Server imagines Customer sitting in toilet guzzling a burger with relish oozing out of the sides, pants round her ankles.

MANAGER (*Laughing insincerely.*) Would you eat your dinner . . . Ha, ha, funny, that's very funny.

To Server.

Who did you think I meant? It's that eejit 'Eric from the Echo'.

To Mother.

Now, if you'd like to follow . . .

MOTHER Perhaps I'd better go.

MANAGER Really! Oh such a shame. I suppose the wee girlie's getting a bit tired now.

MOTHER It's a boy actually.

MANAGER Sorry?

MOTHER The baby, it's a boy.

MANAGER Of course, I should have guessed. Look at those legs – footballing potential if ever I saw it.

MOTHER (*Gathering up her things.*) Do you think so? (*Curt.*)

MANAGER (*To Server.*) Where are our manners? Help the little lady out, will you?

MOTHER No, I'll manage . . . Don't let me *distract* you from your work . . . And by the way, you've overcharged me. I didn't have a 'Sam Fox' shake.

MANAGER (*Looking away from Server.*) Eric!

Close-up on Eric, spivy-looking 'Sun' photographer type.

MANAGER (*To Server.*) Well, don't just stand there, bring him over.

Server's gaze slowly follows Mother as she leaves with baby. As she moves towards the door, the Photographer comes into view under 'Diner Dolls', entrance neon sign in reverse.

PHOTOGRAPHER (*To Mother who is struggling with buggy.*) Lovely baby, lovely – look at that smile. Ever thought about entering him for the 'Bouncing Babe' Competition? I could give you a very nice deal on a 10″×8″, with imitation mahogany frame for no extra charge if you were interested.

MOTHER No, not today thanks.

PHOTOGRAPHER No, well, suit yourself.

He walks away leaving Mother struggling in the background to assemble buggy (one-handedly). Even though the focus is not Mother, we become aware of her growing frustration. She eventually throws the buggy down and buries her head into the baby and cries softly. He walks close up to Server.

PHOTOGRAPHER Manager in, is he? Let's get on with it, shall we? I've got another three of these to do before the pubs open.

He lifts his camera to his face.

I'll just take a couple first to finish off the film. You go and get yourself ready on that table over there. I'll be with you in a minute.

With each click of the camera we see a frozen image of the Customer happily tucking into her 'Tropical Tantaliser'. The last photo shows the Manager smiling broadly at the camera. The Manager 'comes to life'.

We are now observing the drama through the Photographer's eyes.

MANAGER (*To Photographer.*) Eric. Great to see you. We've got the winner this time. The 'Diner Dobbin' pic, fell flat on its face with Head Office. Sales went down 10 per cent over that quarter. All the punters thought they were eating horse meat . . . I've set it up on the table by the door. That way you'll get the name in the picture as well.

He goes to move away, then turns back.

Come round the back when you're done, I've got that wee half-bottle from Christmas.

Photographer's glance moves swiftly over neon strip, and as at beginning, we have a slow fade in on the table under the 'Diner Dolls' light. The angle constantly changing to give the impression of a photographer lining up a shot. 'Addicted to Love' is once again playing in the background. This time more quietly. We hear the Photographer speak this time, even though we don't see him, since we are viewing the scene through his eyes.

As we draw nearer, we see that the Server is perched on the table wearing her 'Diner Dolls' uniform. Very skimpy 'American Flag' sequin shorts with a bikini top made out of imitation 'sesame buns', one bun over each breast. She looks very unhappy.

PHOTOGRAPHER That's it, lovely. Head a little to the right. Beautiful, shoulders back, good, cross your legs, sweetheart, wonderful.

SERVER (*Picking up something from the table.*) She forgot the baby's rattle.

PHOTOGRAPHER Perfect!

As in 1940s detective films, we see the spinning image of a newspaper page. The image freezes and we see final image of the piece. Under the headline 'Diner Doll Dishes Out!' The Server is posed with her thumb in her mouth, holding the baby's rattle to the side of her face.

'Addicted to Love' plays as the credits roll.

The End

The Wake

Jenny McLeod

SCENE 1. INTERIOR. KITCHEN (PRESENT DAY). DAY.
A kitchen with a table and chairs. At the table Frances is decorating the top tier of a wedding cake – there are three tiers. She writes 'Frances and Lucian' on it and places 'The Bride and Groom' on it and then admires it. She then starts making sandwiches: she roughly butters two slices of bread, slaps ham on one and then the other slice of bread. Uncut she places the sandwich on top of a pile of others – she has several large piles – and stands back wondering if she has done enough. Deciding she hasn't, she gets another loaf and throws the empty wrapper on the floor amongst a mass of others. She starts making sandwiches again, humming to herself, and we now become aware of the other things on the table: bottles of alcohol – especially stout – a large white trifle, a rusty old horseshoe and some yellow creased telegrams.

SCENE 2. INTERIOR. LOUNGE (PRESENT DAY). DAY.
Frances looks in a mirror, over the mantel, putting the finishing touches to her lipstick which is a bright red. She ties her headscarf on her head, puts on her gloves and then her coat. She is dressed in black, ready for a funeral. She goes through to the kitchen and returns dish by dish with the food she prepared previously, placing them on a large table. Finally she returns with the trifle and places it beside the cake, in the centre of the table. She picks up her handbag and leaves.

SCENE 3. INTERIOR. LOUNGE (PRESENT DAY). NIGHT.
Frances enters, still in her black clothes. She takes her gloves off and as she speaks removes a picture from a cabinet drawer and a frame from her handbag and fits the picture in it.

FRANCES Well, she's finally gone and done it. Finally gone and died.

Gently she places it dead centre on the mantel and stands admiring it.

And now you're back where you belong. You like the frame? I knew you would. Sixty pence from a nice man on the corner. I had my gloves on and he said 'Just give it a polish now and then Mrs.'. Imagine him knowing I was married.

She touches her rings.

Not many in church. Me, the vicar of course, and some man she'd known. He'd read the obituaries and decided to come. Said he'd known her when they were younger – in the biblical sense too I bet. Said he couldn't come back for tea though since he had a prior engagement. I told him that was fine, since I didn't have a thing in.

She looks at the food.

And the vicar had another do on. Do was his word, but quite appropriate. I don't want you to get jealous, Luci, but he put his arm around me! The vicar put his arm right round me, squeezed and then said one word. 'Cry!' But I couldn't. He's sort of modern and likes touching a lot – reminded me of you.

The clock strikes six. She looks up at it and smiles.

Look at me! What can I be thinking? You'll be in for your tea and nothing done.

SCENE 4. INTERIOR. KITCHEN (1950s). NIGHT.
Frances is in the kitchen, but it's now changed from Scene 1 (it is dated 1950s). She is cutting a thick piece of steak with a large knife. She hears the front door open and then bang shut and she smiles, moving about the kitchen humming. She gets a pan down and starts cooking. Shortly Lucian enters and she stops, staring at him. He is young and good-looking. Her clothes are also dated (1950s). He is in his work clothes: dirty, oily overalls.

FRANCES Won't be long. Had it cut specially. Just the way you like it.

Lucian ignores her. He begins taking his clothes off and stands at the sink in his vest, with overalls around his waist, washing his arms, face and neck. Frances moves to the larder and takes out a bottle of stout with a glass turned down over the top.

Just the way you like it. I chilled the glass too.

She pours it and leaves it on the table. She gets the towel and stands smiling, watching him lather his face and neck. He reaches for the towel blindly and she is there wiping his face softly. He ignores her and moves to the table and begins drinking his stout. Frances follows him and sits beside him. She holds one of his hands looking at it as he raises the glass to his mouth.

You used to have hands that had never seen a day's work. Pretty hands. 'That's the only part of a man a woman likes soft,' remember? You used to make me jealous, telling me about your women and how their husbands were away. You always did like a risk. 'What's life for?' you'd ask. I never could answer. As soon as I saw you dodge that tram on Lambert Street – the front not an inch from taking your leg – I knew. That was the first time I saw you. You didn't notice me. I followed you. You met Carol Simkin. You went to the picture house. I waited in the snow. You both came out laughing. You wanted to kiss her. She wouldn't let you. She made you wait.

Music comes thumping from next door and jolts Frances. Lucian's hand falls away and he disappears.

SCENE 5. INTERIOR. LOUNGE (PRESENT DAY). NIGHT.
Instantly Frances is back in the lounge in the same position as she was: standing looking at the framed picture of Lucian. The set is now in the 1980s. Frances looks up at the clock. It is six o'clock (same time as before). She looks at the wall.

FRANCES She, her next door, she told him straight the other day. 'If you don't like it, you know what you can do.' He didn't answer, he never does. I admire her telling him though. I never did. I've got a way with him. Tommy, her young man. She doesn't like me. Well, he was my young man before hers. I advertised for him, I found him, he came looking for me. Good-looking – just like you, Luci. I watched him walk down the street. He stopped next door at her house. Goes striding up the path, picks up the milk, puts it under his jacket, then rings the bell! She comes with her noisy hi-fi. They say it stands for hi-fidelity, I wouldn't know. Well, Tommy speaks to her. 'Does Ian Smith live here?' Well I thought he lived somewhere in Africa!

She says 'No!' and shuts the door without giving him a second look, and Tommy walks down the path, through the gate and then stops right outside and drinks the milk. He drank the milk! Then he came over to us, Luci. I was ready for him. I answered the door and he says, 'I understand you have a room to rent?' I had to smile, he reminded me so much of you. Then because I had him, she wanted him – women are like that – so he left the room and went to live with her. Now they have a 'relationship!' Not a marriage, a 'relationship!' As if such a thing would have been allowed in our day! He still comes though. I make him a proper steak dinner or a cake – just like you, Luci. And she's jealous. Thinks there's something where there's nothing. He could be my grandson . . . but you need children to have grands don't you?

Looking at the food.

We had a big spread like this at our wedding didn't we, Luci? Almost as big as me at six months in a white three-tier wedding dress. You ate all the trifle and ended up sick. You just sat there like thunder, stuffed yourself, then rushed out and vomited. I rushed after you. You didn't look like you. You didn't look pretty and young – like my Luci. You looked sick. Then mother came. She sent me away. Your mouth needed wiping and she sent me away. Said she'd wipe your mouth. She'd wash your face. She'd clean you up. She'd make you better!

The music stops. Frances looks at the wall. Then it comes on again.

She can go on for hours when she gets going. Usually to annoy me. She wears trousers a lot. I've never worn a pair . . . Lots of make-up that makes her eyes bigger than they are and bright red blood lipstick. You always used to say 'You can't help kissing a woman wearing blood lipstick.'

Frances smacks her lips.

She's very intelligent, got a degree and everything. Mathematics, Tommy said. But the oddest thing, I don't know her name. First I thought it was Sheila, because he always used to say, 'She this and She that.' So one day I said, 'Tell Sheila to . . .' And he said 'Sheila who?' Tommy says they argue – as if I couldn't work that out. Said he didn't know what was going wrong. What he could do to make things right. She thinks it's me. Thinks I come between them, but I don't. At least not on purpose. Why would I want to? Of course he confides in me, not quite the way you used to in mother, Luci, but she's putting too much store in our friendship. It's how Tommy is, he likes chat. And anyway, I think he spends too much time with her, it's not healthy. Something always comes between them though, someone. . . I used to think she wasn't my mother. I tried to get her to admit it. Say she adopted me: stole me from my frilly pink pram. . . Remember the first time mother met you, Luci? You were walking up the path – just like Tommy. I was looking out, wondering when you'd come and then you were there. 'He's here, Mother. Luci's here.' She didn't answer.

I said it again, 'He's here, Mother. Luci's here.' She couldn't answer. She just stood there staring; standing there staring she was, and at my Luci too! Everything in her head stopped and her eyes made you move so slow, your feet got stuck in treacle. Then she had to change, put on a clean dress, do her hair. . . You came to me. You were my young man. You brought her flowers. Only to impress her, but she pressed them in a book and kept them until she died.

The music suddenly stops, she goes to the wall and puts her ear to it.

That's odd.

She listens for a bit.

Oh. They're at it.

She moves away from the wall.

He should be over for his tea. I did invite him.

SCENE 6. INTERIOR. LOUNGE (PRESENT DAY). NIGHT.
Frances asleep on the sofa, the clock strikes half past eight, she wakes
up. She puts the light on and looks at the clock and then the wall.
She listens at the wall. Goes to the table and brushes the table cloth,
fixes a fork – generally fussing around the table.

FRANCES You're starting to leave me out again. And after all we said. I
wish I knew when it started. Physically, I mean. I'd like to know the
second, but I can't even suppose the day. I remember when father
died. I was two months married. Heart attack, 1952. He looked at
me, said I should leave. Move out. Me and Lucian. Wasn't healthy
a married woman living with her mother. I asked him what he
meant. 'It wasn't healthy!' Lucian should provide a home. He got
Lucian the mechanic's job. Lucian hated getting his hands dirty
and father knew. 'Pretty hands, that hadn't seen a day's work.' You
were funny that way, always washing and grooming. Weren't you,
Luci?

SCENE 7. INTERIOR. LOUNGE (1950s). NIGHT.
Lucian enters – the scene changes to 1950s – wet with a towel
around him and another drying his hair. He rushes to the coal fire
and stands before it shivering and warming himself. The room is a
glowing warm orange. He sits on the hearth, shaking his wet hair
at the fire and then begins combing it wet. Frances moves to him,
smiling and touching his hair as he combs it.

FRANCES I opened the door. Only a little bit and then a little bit more
and there you were fast asleep with your head on her sagging large
breast. Your hair was wet, and straight away I wanted to touch it. . .

Frances strokes his hair.

I wanted to stroke it. . . But I didn't.

*She stops stroking his hair and stares at him combing it and towel-
ling it.*

I felt like an intruder.

Frances still on her knees, now stares into the burning fire.

I closed the door and I never had anyone to talk to again. I went to
the coal-house and had her. She wouldn't cry, I wanted her to cry,

move, something, but she wouldn't. As big as my hand. That's all she was. I wiped her clean with my apron. We were going to call her Lucile, Lucy for short. I said you'd both come running when I called, I thought that would be nice. But you never knew, I called her Rosey instead. In the coal-house, she just looked like a Rosey. She wouldn't cry, I wanted her to cry. I wanted you to come. Help me, tell me what to do, make her cry, and you had your head on my mother's breast, you had my husband in your bed.

> SCENE 8. INTERIOR. LOUNGE (PRESENT DAY). NIGHT.
> *Sounds of children playing come in from outside, which jolt Frances. Lucian has gone – the scene changes back – the fire has gone and Frances is before the empty hearth.*

FRANCES I remember that now, I remember children playing in the alley and my Rosey still.

> SCENE 9. INTERIOR. LOUNGE (PRESENT DAY). MORNING.
> *Frances looking out of the window searching. She looks at the clock on the mantel, goes to the wall, listens, hears a door slam, then dashes back to the window and smiles.*

FRANCES There she goes. Tommy should be over for his breakfast now. I knew there was a reason he didn't come yesterday.

> *She takes a card out of her pocket and reads.*

'Sorry about yesterday, got caught up, pop over this morning and tell you about it. Tommy.'

> *She looks at the card and smiles.*

Was on the door step when I went for the milk. And a bunch of flowers.

> *She looks at the flowers in a vase on the mantel.*

Never seen him buy them for her.

> *The sound of a van is heard outside. Frances goes to the window and looks out.*

Tommy never said they were having new furniture. But that's probably what he's coming in to tell me. Tells me everything.

The clock strikes nine.

Look at me! What can I be thinking? You'll be in for your breakfast and nothing done.

Frances exits to the kitchen, humming.

SCENE 10. INTERIOR. LOUNGE (PRESENT DAY). NIGHT.
Frances looking at the vase of flowers and the card beside it. On a tray is a plate of breakfast: eggs, bacon, sausages, etc. The sandwiches from yesterday have curled and she tries straightening a few out.

FRANCES Tommy said he'd pop in and he did. Just like he said.

She's still looking at the food.

Asked me if I was having a party. Said it would do me good to have a few friends round and how was it he's never met any of my friends? Kept saying what a tonic I'd been to him when he and she were going through that bad patch a while back. Said 'he'd always remember me.' I asked him what he meant, 'he'd always remember me?' He wanted to thank me – he'd brought me more flowers.

Besides the vase of flowers is another bunch of flowers still in their wrapping.

Kept saying he wanted to thank me. Pushed them right in my face. 'You'll be spoiling me,' I said. 'You deserve it more than anyone I know.' Then he said it again, 'He'd always remember me. Never forget me. . .' His door banged shut and he smiled, said he had to go, she was back. He put his arm around me, squeezed and then kissed me. On the cheek. And left. The removal van didn't take long. Well, they hadn't got much of their own. I watched Tommy jump in beside the driver and then she got in. She waved at me, grinning. I dropped the curtain.

SCENE 11. INTERIOR. LOUNGE (1950s). DAY.
*Lucian enters – scene changes to 1950s – dressed in a suit, brushing
bits off and fussing over himself.*

FRANCES Oh, you do look smart. You going out?

*He ignores her, puts his foot up on the table, next to the wedding
cake, and begins polishing his already shiny black boot, then the
other one. He raises up, looks in the mirror over the mantel and
smooths back his hair. Frances tries fixing his collar and tie, but he
shrugs her away.*

You go off. Don't mind me. I've plenty to do.

Lucian picks up his suitcase and leaves.

You know me. Always busy. . . Then mother comes down. I said
'Oh, Mother, you do look smart. You going out? You go off. Don't
mind me. I've plenty to do. You know me. Always busy.' Then she
looks in the mirror, and smiles fixing her hair. Picks up her suitcase
and leaves.

SCENE 12. INTERIOR. LOUNGE (PRESENT DAY). NIGHT.

FRANCES I never told you how she came back, did I, Luci? Less than a
month since you both left it was. I walked up the path one evening
and there she was, on the door step, just sitting there on her case. It
was pouring. She didn't have a coat or anything, just a fur thing
round her neck. She stood up when she saw me. Picked up her case
and stood there dead straight – well, as straight as she could with
one heel broken. She was wearing a red dress. It was too small and
the rain made it worse; made it cling to her and then that fur thing
round her neck. . . The rain was rolling off her lashes and into her
eyes, and when she blinked it seemed like she was crying. Her
blood lipstick was smudged and it seemed as if she had plastered it
from ear to ear. She didn't say a thing. Just followed me in when I
opened the door. She thinks Tommy'll marry her, put a ring on her
finger, stick by her.

*Frances picks up a note pad off the table and starts writing. She
finishes and puts it on the table. It says 'Wanted. Young man of
twenty-two to rent room in the home of a middle-aged woman. Good
home cooking/all meals provided. Must be good-looking.'*
The End

A Box of Swan

Alan David Price

SCENE 1. INTERIOR. HEALTH FOOD SHOP. DAY.
John picks up a loaf of unsliced fresh bread and smells it.

SCENE 2. EXTERIOR. HIGH STREET. DAY.
*A dull, wet summer day. John walks quickly. Stops. Goes to bite
bread. Stops. Continues walking.*

SCENE 3. EXTERIOR. FUNERAL SERVICE ROOMS. DAY.
*John rings the bell. Door opens. An undertaker's assistant stares
suspiciously. He is young, greasy-haired, squint in one eye.*

JOHN Is this the chapel of rest? I've come to see my father.
ASSISTANT What's the name?
JOHN Alfred Morris.

The assistant lets John in.

SCENE 4. INTERIOR. FUNERAL SERVICE ROOMS: CHAPEL OF REST. DAY.
Music: Elgar/Sospiri.

*Father's body lies in coffin. A few wreaths on floor. Door opens. John
enters. He sighs. Smells bread. Places it on chair. Then touches
Father's forehead, the bread and his own forehead. Repeats this
instinctively. A quasi-religious act.*

JOHN God bless you!

John bends over Father. Hesitates to kiss him. Goes over to bread.
Tears off a piece and chews it. John turns to face Father.

JOHN You're looking bloody great. Tony cleaned your suit up well. We can't have you looking scruffy.

SCENE 5. *FLASHBACK. INTERIOR. PARENTS' COUNCIL FLAT: LIVING ROOM.*
NIGHT.

Music: Elgar/Sospiri.

MOTHER 'Ave you washed yer face?
FATHER Course I 'ave.
MOTHER Yer look very grey to me.
FATHER Don't be silly.

SCENE 6. *INTERIOR. FUNERAL SERVICE ROOMS: CHAPEL OF REST. DAY.*

Music: Elgar/Sospiri.

John gently strokes his father's face.

SCENE 7. *FLASHBACK. EXTERIOR. STREET. DAY.*
Close shot of Father's live (dirty) face. Father stands next to road-sweeper's cart. He brushes the street. Stops. Picks up a twopence coin from the gutter. Spits on coin. Cleans it. Close shot of coin in Father's palm.

FATHER (*Voice over.*) 'Ere's something for yer!

Hand covers coin.

Music: Elgar/Sospiri.

SCENE 8. *FLASHBACK. INTERIOR. PARENTS' COUNCIL FLAT: LIVING ROOM.*
NIGHT.

Music: Elgar/Sospiri.

Shot of closed hand. Then opened. More money in Father's palm.
Father – dirty and dishevelled-looking – offers John the money.

FATHER All the small change I've got.
JOHN And the rest! You've loads of money hoarded away!
FATHER (*Not listening.*) 'Ere are!

JOHN Eighty-one pence. Don't insult me. I'm not a child!

FATHER (*Hurt.*) I thought it would help you out for getting back to London.

Abrupt silencing of music.

SCENE 9. INTERIOR. FUNERAL SERVICE ROOMS: CHAPEL OF REST. DAY. John places hands on sides of coffin. Leans over Father. Tries to shake the coffin.

JOHN All you did was repeat silly questions. Do yer live near Big Ben? How long does it take on the train back to London? Do yer cook for yourself? Eighty-one pence. Nineteen off a pound!

Assistant knocks on door.

JOHN Come in.

Assistant enters. Embarrassed.

ASSISTANT I'm sorry. It's one o'clock.

JOHN You need to get him ready for the three-twenty start.

ASSISTANT Three-twenty-five!

John picks up bread and grips it very tightly. He looks far away.

Pause.

Assistant nervously combs hair with hand.

I'm sorry but we have to close for lunch.

John distractedly breaks off a piece of bread and chews it. Glances at wreaths.

JOHN Nice wreaths. Not many. He didn't make friends . . . nice wreaths!

He tears off more bread and offers it to the assistant. Assistant feels awkward. John tries to relax hold on bread.

He held on to everything.

SCENE 10. EXTERIOR. PARK GATES. DAY.
*John deliberately squeezes the bread against his ribs. Then angrily
hurls it over park gates.*

JOHN Aaargh!

Music: Elgar/Sospiri.

*Climax of music's arching theme mixed with park scene montage.
Shot of bread on grass. John kicks it like a football. Shot of edge of
park lake. John taps bread with foot. Shot of nearby swan.
Unruffled. Watching. John is poised to kick bread into lake. Close
shot of swan. Dissolve to close-up of box of Swan Vesta matches. Its
swan design bobbing on lake. The name Alfred Morris has been
scrawled underneath picture.*

MOTHER (*Voice over.*) I don't know! . . . What do you do with your life?

SCENE 11. FLASHBACK. INTERIOR. PARENTS' COUNCIL FLAT: LIVING ROOM.
NIGHT.

*Seated Father sucks unlit pipe. Feet up on stool . . . Mother seated
in high invalid's chair. TV is on. BBC quiz programme. Room is
small and crowded with furniture.*

FATHER Eh?

MOTHER You never spend a penny on me. Or bother to take us out!

*Shot of Father striking match on Swan Vesta box. He lights pipe.
Billows out smoke.*

FATHER What's there to go out for?

*Father places dead match with others – lying on small, cloth-covered
table. Table is jammed against wheels of folded wheelchair. Angled
in corner. Unused.*

MOTHER I need some exercise. Take me to the bench near the road!

FATHER It's a terrible summer.

MOTHER Not even the sun will shift your arse!

Father writes on the match box. Door opening. John enters room.

MOTHER Did you have a nice evening out?

JOHN Yes . . . I could do with a cup of tea.

Father throws over box of matches.

FATHER (*Generously.*) We'll all 'ave a cup!

John catches them. He notices writing on box.

JOHN God, do yer still write yer name on a box of Swan? You were doing this when I was a child!

Father suddenly gets up and changes channel on TV.

MOTHER That's the tenth time he's changed it tonight. Just can't concentrate!

SCENE 12. EXTERIOR. PARK LAKE. DAY.

John kicks the bread into lake. It splashes near swan.

FATHER (*Voice over.*) Shut up, you two. It's me only bit of pleasure!

*For a second, swan and man eye each other up. It starts to rain.
John turns up jacket collar. He walks away.*

SCENE 13. THE PRESENT. INTERIOR. PARENTS' COUNCIL FLAT: KITCHEN. DAY.

*Tony – John's elder brother – is cleaning a kitchen cabinet. John
enters. Picks up teatowel and dries his hair.*

TONY Dad never kept the place clean.

JOHN Cleaning! He could only handle that in his job.

Shot of Father's handprint on side of cabinet. Tony rubs harder.

TONY Responsibilities!

Shot of John drying his hair harder.

JOHN Like bringing up his children!

TONY Damn! . . . should have bought some sugar soap!

FATHER (*Voice over.*) Yer don't need that . . . expensive! Washing-up liquid will do!

JOHN (*Sighing.*) It seems to be coming off. Give it time!

SCENE 14. INTERIOR. PARENTS' COUNCIL FLAT: LIVING ROOM. DAY.
John stands by the door. He watches Mother staring out of window.
She turns round.

MOTHER Where have you been?
JOHN To see Dad.
MOTHER How did he look?
JOHN Pretty good.
MOTHER I couldn't have *faced* seeing him.

Pause.

Three days before he died he suddenly said that he loved me. He
was talking soft!
JOHN Soft . . . ?

SCENE 15. FANTASY. INTERIOR. FUNERAL SERVICE ROOM: CHAPEL OF REST.
DAY.
Funeral assistant raises Father's body. Final funeral arrange-
ment.

FATHER (*Voice over.*) I love you. But you never loved me, did you?

Body is rested in coffin. Assistant puts on lid.

SCENE 16. INTERIOR. PARENTS' COUNCIL FLAT: LIVING ROOM. DAY.

JOHN Did you really love him?
MOTHER To be honest . . . no!
JOHN Why? . . . why?

Mother begins to cry. Tony enters room.

TONY Did yer get any bread for the sandwiches, John?
JOHN I forgot . . . I mean . . .
TONY (*Angry.*) Christ, there's still so many arrangements!
JOHN (*Controlling himself.*) I'll get us a large white sliced.
TONY Yes . . . not your health food stuff!
MOTHER Where's my purse?
JOHN (*Angry.*) Dad's dead. We don't need your money now!

SCENE 17. EXTERIOR. THE CEMETERY. DAY.
A windy afternoon. Father's coffin is lowered into its grave by four bearers. Mother and sons approach them. Mother walks with walking frame. The priest closes Bible. He throws dirt on to the coffin. Sons pick up small mounds of dirt – neatly prepared for them. John and Tony throw their dirt. Mother is not sure whether to pick up dirt or not. John hands it to her.

MOTHER Shall I move closer? I can't see yer Dad from here.
JOHN You're close enough.

Mother weakly throws dirt. It only lands on side of grave.

MOTHER Can't see what I'm doin'. I feel so cold.

Tony hands her some more dirt. John looks resentful.

TONY A bit harder!

Mother throws again.

SCENE 18. EXTERIOR. THE CEMETERY. DAY.
Music: Elgar/Sospiri.

Inside the grave. No coffin but a small, white cardboard box. Picture on box of a woman's bust wearing a bra – number 38. Dirt is thrown on to box. Wind blows off the dirt, then the loose box lid. Inside is an untidy pile of bank notes. Money is blown out of box. It swirls round in grave. A trapped air pocket.

JOHN (*Voice over.*) Father left one thousand, six hundred and eighty-nine pounds, thirty-five pence.
MOTHER (*Voice over.*) I didn't know.
JOHN (*Voice over.*) It was hidden behind the kitchen cabinet. Inside a cardboard box that you kept your prosthesis in.
MOTHER (*Voice over.*) Me what?
JOHN (*Voice over.*) Your false breast.
MOTHER (*Voice over.*) Oh yes . . . I take size 38.
JOHN (*Voice over.*) He also had building society savings.

SCENE 19. INTERIOR. PARENTS' COUNCIL FLAT: KITCHEN. DAY.
*Mother, John, Tony and his wife, Patricia, are eating sandwiches,
drinking whisky.*

MOTHER I never . . .

JOHN You're well off now.

MOTHER Am I? I really need a better pair of legs.

JOHN Legs were always too expensive!

MOTHER Never mind. God's good.

PATRICIA (*Coming over.*) I never knew you drank spirits, John!

JOHN A secret habit of your brother-in-law!

PATRICIA You never visit us enough for us to know yer ways!

Tension is set up between John and Patricia.

TONY Eleven years living in London!

JOHN (*Relieved it's been longer.*) Twelve!

MOTHER He's well out of Liverpool. There's nothing going on here.

PATRICIA (*Put out.*) It's not that bad!

She addresses John.

What are you doing now?

JOHN Designing a hotel.

PATRICIA We could do with an architect. Build us a better house!

JOHN I don't do houses.

PATRICIA (*Enviously.*) I bet you live in a smart one!

Pause.

TONY Let's not stay in tonight. How about a Greek restaurant?

MOTHER Oh . . . I don't know.

JOHN (*Surprised.*) It's a great idea.

Patricia has to interrupt. Thrusts cigarette out.

PATRICIA Give me a light!

SCENE 20. INTERIOR. GREEK RESTAURANT. NIGHT.
The family reads the menu.

TONY Mother, what will you have?

MOTHER You choose for me.

PATRICIA Try a steak.
JOHN Moussaka would be best.
MOTHER What's that?
JOHN Mince, cheese, potato, pepper . . . very soft.
MOTHER God, my teeth!
PATRICIA (*Sarcastic.*) John knows about foreign food!

The Greek waiter collects the menus. Patricia wants to laugh.

PATRICIA Did you get a whiff of his after-shave?
TONY (*Laughing.*) Hey, Dimitrios!
PATRICIA 'E was eyeing up John.
TONY They're all bent in Corfu!

Tony, Patricia and Mother – who doesn't fully understand – laugh loudly. John feels uncomfortable. He glances at end of table. Father is sitting there.

FATHER Yer don't want that!

SCENE 21. INTERIOR. GREEK RESTAURANT. NIGHT.
Some time later. Family are eating. Beginning to 'relax'.

JOHN (*Voice over.*) First meal out we've ever had . . . together!

Shot of Mother eating.

JOHN (*Voice over.*) Father decided your life. *I* can't help you!

Shot of Tony eating.

JOHN (*Voice over.*) Ten years older than me. I missed you when I was growing up.

Shot of Patricia eating.

JOHN (*Voice over.*) Who are you? Why are you here?

John looks up from meal. He stares at Father seated at end of table. Smoking his pipe. Dirty. Dishevelled. Behind him is his road-sweeper's brush and cart.

FATHER Yer don't want them, John. You're like me. We never belonged.

Father points his pipe at Mother.

FATHER I wanted her, but . . . Eh, John, what time's your train back to London. Do yer live very far from the Houses of Parliament? Can you build ordinary houses like the ones in our street?

JOHN (*Painfully.*) Is that all then? . . . answer me!

PATRICIA (*To Tony.*) A roadsweeper. Yer Dad could have done a better job.

TONY Somebody's got to do it.

MOTHER 'E did it for twenty-seven years.

JOHN Have some more Retsina, Mother!

PATRICIA Who's bloody Retsina when she's at home!

TONY Shut up!

John fills his mother's glass.

JOHN We ought to toast him.

MOTHER Who?

JOHN (*Angry.*) Father!

They all toast Father.

Music: Elgar/Sospiri.

Lights darken round family group. Only the table is lit. Each member of the family disappears. First Mother and Tony. Patricia is smoking. Places box of matches on table. She disappears. John toys with box. Puts it down. Places tip on table. He disappears. Greek waiter begins to clear the table. He goes to pick up tip of one pound coin. Hand freezes.

FATHER (*Voice over.*) Yer don't want to leave that!

Father pockets the tip.

Music: Elgar/Sospiri.

Musical arch of theme soars over final images. Shots of box of Swan Vesta matches. Box bursts into flames. Close-up of burning swan. Close-up of Father's face.

Fade out.

The End.